SIMPLICITY FROM A MONASTERY KITCHEN

# SIMPLICITY FROM A MONASTERY KITCHEN

## A COMPLETE MENU COOKBOOK
## FOR ALL OCCASIONS

### BROTHER VICTOR-ANTOINE D'AVILA-LATOURRETTE

Broadway Books

New York

Broadway Books titles may be purchased for business or promotional use or for special sales. For information please write to: Special Markets Department, Random House, Inc., 1540 Broadway, New York, NY 10036.

BROADWAY BOOKS and its logo, a letter B bisected on the diagonal, are trademarks of Broadway Books, a division of Random House, Inc.

Visit our website at www.broadway books.com

Library of Congress Cataloging-in-Publication Data
D'Avila-Latourrette, Victor-Antoine.
    Simplicity from a monastery kitchen: a complete menu cookbook for all occasions/
Victor-Antoine D'Avila-Latourrette.—1st ed.
        p. cm.
    Includes index.
    1. Vegetarian cookery.    I. Title.
TX837.D2724 2001
641.5'636—dc21                                                                    00-066769

FIRST EDITION

Designed by Songhee Kim

ISBN 0-7679-0609-8

01   02   03   04   05   10   9   8   7   6   5   4   3   2   1

# Contents

# Introduction

Simplicity is a cherished virtue in monastic life. It is part of its very essence. Simplicity is closely aligned with truth, for it allows us to deal directly with the ordinariness of daily events and see them in their true reality. Simplicity embraces truth and tries to escape as far as possible from falsehood, complexity, multiplicity, tensions, conflict, division, and all that ultimately leads to destruction.

The original Greek word for monk is *monachos,* which means the man that is alone, one in himself, single-minded, simple. In entering monastic life, the monk deliberately embraces the way of simplicity and promises to seek God throughout his life in true simplicity of heart. His monastic journey, therefore, consists essentially of a constant effort to attain this perfect simplicity by letting go of the clutter and accumulations of the past and by opening himself intimately and solely to the reality of the present moment. In connecting with the present moment, the monk discovers within himself the inner harmony of true simplicity, for it is in this transparent simplicity of the present moment that he encounters the living God.

Authentic simplicity, as commanded and inspired by the Gospel, demands asceticism and spiritual effort on the part of every Christian and hence of the monk. It demands the practice of self-renunciation and the letting go of all forms of worldly illusion. Practiced this way, monastic simplicity becomes the antithesis to the falsehood of the ways of the world. While the wisdom of the world stresses the glorification and exaltation of the self, monastic simplicity finds its purpose in the practice of humility and frugality that frees the human heart for the love of God and His Kingdom.

It is of the very essence of monastic simplicity that the inner spiritual life and the practical ordinary tasks of daily life be woven by the same thread. Since it is the same faith that inspires every moment and every act of the monastic existence, a dichotomy between what is purely spiritual and what is more secular or mundane in character would be considered artificial and totally incompatible in monastic life. People who visit monasteries are sometimes surprised seeing the monks or nuns occupied with such trivia as milking cows, feeding the chickens, weeding the gardens, scrubbing the floors, baking the daily bread, and so on. They imagine them always at prayers in the church, singing chants or reading in the library or in the solitude of their cells. They are astonished to discover that for these monks and nuns, prayer and work do not conflict with each other. Instead, they are simply two distinct parcels of the same entity. Slowly visitors begin to realize that the simplicity and unity of monastic life is woven throughout all of that life's events, whether they be liturgical or private prayer, manual or intellectual work, spiritual reading or chanting, practicing hospitality or living in the strictest of solitudes, shearing sheep or cooking in the kitchen. What may seem an apparent conflict to the secular eye, it is a source of unity to the monk. The monk's sole concern remains that "God be glorified in all things," as counseled by Saint Benedict.

The daily rhythm of monastic life attaches great importance to the time spent in the kitchen and food preparation, to time in the refectory and the act of consuming food. Saint Benedict attached great importance to these matters, and throughout the whole of monastic tradition, food retained a sacred character, because of the importance given to it by Christ Himself. Anyone participating today in the life of a monastery notices the importance the monks and nuns give to their meals, their practical and healthy method of cooking, and their reverential way of serving food at the table and their equally reverent consumption of it. The meal, depending on the season of the year (fasting or nonfasting), day of the week, or celebration, may consist of several courses, prepared and served in great simplicity, but always enhanced by a tradition of good taste cultivated in monasteries throughout the centuries.

Across the ages monastic cooking, both in the Christian and non-Christian tradition (Buddhist, Hindu, and so on) has distinguished itself from other forms of cooking, for their simplicity, frugality, balance, wholesomeness, and flavor. Monastic cooking entails much more than the just plain preparation of ordinary good food. For instance, the monastery cook works in collaboration with the monks in charge of the kitchen gardens, and he relies on their help in order to assure the quality and freshness of the produce presented at the table. The same close collaboration takes place between him and the monk's farmer, who helps provide the eggs, the milk, the butter, and the cheese consumed at the monastic table. At the beginning of his formation the future monastic cook is apprenticed to an older, more experienced monk cook. This is so that he may be properly trained and learn from the wise experience of the elder. It usually takes years of experience and much imagination before the new cook is able to develop creative, delicious, and well-balanced meals on his own. To arrive at this point, it takes a certain experience and also a creative thriftiness, which indeed, is very monastic.

The recipes presented in this book reflect the experience of a simple monastic cuisine, in particular, the cuisine at Our Lady of the Resurrection. In my experience as a monk and cookbook author, I have at times been criticized for the extreme bare simplicity of my recipes, but more often have been congratulated for it. I do not know how many people have told me again and again that they were afraid to engage themselves in the art of cooking because of its apparent complexity and were greatly helped by the rudimentariness of my recipes, which they said helped them overcome their fears and gave them new confidence. In response, I always encouraged these people to stick with the ways of simplicity in the kitchen, for simplicity itself is synonymous with elegance and good taste. Some of the most elegant, attractive, and appetizing dishes I have ever eaten have been prepared in humble monastery kitchens or in plain country farm kitchens, which sometimes lacked the latest, more expensive technological tools used in modern kitchens. But the cooks in these kitchens had something else going for them. They were creative, efficient, and highly industrious about how they prepared and arranged their dishes. Moreover, they cooked with unaffected skill and great simplicity, with great joy and loving care. The result was food of outstanding quality that brought utter delight to the eye, to the palate, and to the soul.

In presenting these time-tested recipes to the public, my sincere hope is that the reader who is eager to experiment in the kitchen will discover the deep satisfaction inherent in preparing recipes that are guided by the two important principles emphasized here: good quality and wholesome simplicity. I encourage the cook to experiment, improve, and even make certain changes, if necessary, but keep in mind never to sacrifice the principles of quality and simplicity that are the guiding light of this particular cuisine.

In completing this Introduction I wish to thank my editor at Doubleday, Trace Murphy, who strongly supported me in the undertaking of this work. I wish to thank also the many friends in France, Quebec, and here in the U.S.A. who encouraged me and enlighten me along the way. I wish to thank Brother Peter Michael Preble, Sister Ana M. Martinez, and her mother, all of whom patiently typed these recipes. And last but not least, many thanks to our dear friends John and Susan Conrad for typing the Introduction.

My ultimate wish and hope is that these recipes with the accompanying quotations go a long way to inspire many to cook and to walk in the ways of simplicity.

Brother Victor-Antoine, monk
September 14, 1999
Feast of the Holy and Glorious Cross of Christ

## How to Use This Cookbook

The preparation of a dinner, be it either the daily ordinary one or a festal one for a special occasion, can demand a great deal of time and energy. This is true in a home, in a monastery, or even for the person who lives alone. It is indispensable, then, that the meals be well planned ahead of time.

In planning a meal, one must first be guided by the two elementary principles of quality and simplicity that I emphasized in the Introduction. In addition, one must make sure that the meal is balanced, tasty, nutritious, and certainly, economically reasonable. The use of fresh seasonal ingredients is absolutely a must.

This book follows a different method of presenting the recipes from my previous cookbooks, which tended to follow the seasonal or monthly calendar. Here, instead, I chose to follow the principle of grouping the recipes according to the category to which they belong. For instance, if one is looking for a soup recipe, one will look for it under the soup category. If one is thinking of preparing an egg dish, then one will look for it under the egg dishes category. A keen eye will always easily find an interesting recipe that can satisfy both his or her sense of adventure in the kitchen and, more important yet, the pleasures of his or her palate.

Depending on the time available to the cook, the season, and the particular occasion for the meal (a festive one or an ordinary everyday one), I recommend the following way of choosing the recipes for a meal.

For the daily ordinary cuisine I will tend to follow this method and offer the following courses at the table:

1. Soup (especially during cold months)
2. Main course
   —Choose between a casserole or rice or pasta dish
   —Or choose between an egg or fish dish
   —If eggs or fish (or meat for nonvegetarians) are chosen, use as an accompaniment a recipe from the vegetables or mushrooms section.

3. A fresh salad course is always welcome.
4. Plain fruit or a very simple, basic dessert, depending on the season. For instance, a warm dessert is always appetizing in winter.

For a special or festive occasion I recommend the following courses:

1. Hors d'oeuvre, appetizer, or salad
2. a. Choice of egg or fish dishes (or meat) accompanied by one or two vegetables from their section, one vegetable and one of mushroom, from their respective sections. (A vegetable pancake would be a nice choice.)
   b. Choice of a crepe dish or one from the rice section, such as Risotto or a Mediterranean Vegetarian Paella.
3. An appetizing salad dish, except when one is served as an appetizer.
4. A festive dessert.

Use sauces as needed to enhance certain vegetables, fish, and other dishes. Use homemade bread to enrich your meals whenever you can.

## THREE MENUS OF AN ORDINARY WEEKLY MEAL

| Spring | Autumn | Winter |
|---|---|---|
| Spring Spinach Soup | Monastery Harvest Soup | Spicy Lentil Soup |
| Potato Omelet Basque Style | Rigatoni with Eggplants | Polenta Savoyarde with |
| Parsnips and Carrots Exupery | Plain Green Salad | Zucchini Beignets |
| Hudson Valley Salad | Pear Flan | Grated Carrots and |
| Melon with Strawberry | | Black Olive Salad |
| and Raspberry | | Country-Style Compote |

| Spring and Summer | Autumn and Winter |
|---|---|
| Melon with Yogurt and Fresh Mint | Eggplant Terrine |
| Ratatouille Crepes with | Rodez Codfish with Potatoes |
| Spanish Lima Beans | Mushrooms à la Bordelaise |
| Provençal Mesclun Salad with Goat Cheese | Apple, Endive, and Celery Root Salad |
| St. Scholastica Peach Tarte | Empress Eugénie Rice Pudding |

Of course, these are only suggestions on how to go about arranging a menu. I leave it to the talent and inventiveness of the cook the task of choosing a tasty and well-balanced meal.

I

HORS D'OEUVRE AND APPETIZERS

# Asparagus Canapés

6 slices whole wheat bread
12–14 asparagus spears
5 tablespoons butter
1/3 cup finely chopped fresh parsley

Salt and freshly ground black
   pepper to taste
2 ounces grated mozzarella cheese
   (or Gruyère)

24 CANAPÉS

1. Preheat the oven to 250°. Cut each bread slice at the center into four even parts (the size of a cracker).
2. Boil the asparagus about 4 minutes, drain them, cut them into 1-inch lengths, and set them aside.
3. Place the butter in a bowl and cream it with the help of a fork. Add the chopped parsley, salt, and pepper, and mix well all the ingredients until a creamy even consistency is achieved.
4. Spread the butter-parsley mixture evenly over each bread slice. Place the sliced bread on a buttered cookie sheet.
5. Cover the top of the bread slices evenly with the asparagus pieces. Add the grated cheese on top of the asparagus. Place the sheet into the oven for 6–8 minutes until the cheese is melted. Serve the canapés hot.

# Canapés à la Provençale

5 slices good peasant bread (or a
    grainy-type brown bread)
4 tablespoons butter
2 tablespoons extra-virgin olive oil
1½ tablespoons herbes de Provence
Salt and freshly ground black
    pepper to taste

2 tablespoons olive oil
1 small onion, sliced
1 garlic clove, finely minced
15 mushrooms, thinly sliced
Grated Parmesan cheese

20 CANAPÉS

1. Preheat the oven to 300°. Slice the crust edges of the bread and discard them. Cut each slice into four even portions.
2. Place the butter in a bowl, add the olive oil, herbes de Provence, salt, and pepper. Mix and cream well all the ingredients with a fork until the mixture reaches an even, creamy consistency. Set it aside.
3. Pour 2 tablespoons olive oil into a skillet and add the onion, garlic, and sliced mushrooms. Sauté lightly for about 3 minutes.
4. Butter thoroughly a cookie sheet or some ovenproof plates. Spread the butter-herb mixture on the bread slices and place them on the cookie sheet or plates.
5. Distribute evenly the onion-mushroom mixture over the top of each small slice. Sprinkle some grated Parmesan cheese on the top. Place the canapés in the oven for about 6 to 8 minutes. Serve them immediately after.

# Canapés with Roquefort and Walnuts

1 baguette or ficelle loaf (long
   french bread)
2 ounces Roquefort cheese,
   crumbled

1½ tablespoons Cognac
1½ tablespoons french mustard
1½ cups walnuts

24 CANAPÉS

1. Preheat the oven to 300°. Cut the baguette into twenty-four even slices. Butter thoroughly a cookie sheet or long ovenproof dish and place the slices there.
2. Place the crumbled Roquefort cheese into a bowl; add the Cognac and mustard. With a fork mix well all the ingredients in the bowl until an even, creamy consistency is achieved. With a knife spread evenly this mixture over the bread slices.
3. In a saucepan boil the walnuts in water to cover for about 5 minutes, until they are softened. Drain the walnuts, place them on paper towels, and then chop them with a sharp knife.
4. Distribute evenly the chopped walnuts over the cheese spread. Place in the oven for about 6 minutes. Transfer them to a serving plate and serve them hot.

INNER SIMPLICITY MEANS CREATING

JOY IN OUR LIVES AND REMEMBERING

TO STAY CONNECTED WITH THAT JOY

EVERY MOMENT OF THE DAY. IT

MEANS LETTING GO OF THE TRAUMAS

THAT KEEP US FROM BEING THE BEST

WE CAN BE.

ELAINE ST. JAMES

# St. Andrew's Stuffed Avocados

2 ripe avocados, unpeeled
1 ripe tomato, chopped into very
    small chunks
1 celery stalk, from the heart or
    center of the celery, finely
    chopped and minced
20 pignoli nuts
1 shallot, finely chopped and
    minced

2 teaspoons tomato paste
3 tablespoons lemon juice
1 tablespoon olive oil
Salt and freshly ground black
    pepper to taste
4 large lettuce leaves
Finely chopped cilantro, as garnish

4 SERVINGS

1. Just before serving, cut each avocado at the center in two even parts.
   Remove the seed.
2. In a bowl place the tomato, celery, nuts, shallot, tomato paste, lemon
   juice, olive oil, salt, and pepper, and mix well. Check the seasonings.
   (Keep it cool until ready to use.)
3. Place a lettuce leaf in each of four serving plates. Put an avocado half
   on top of each leaf. Fill the avocado halves with the mixture from the
   bowl. Sprinkle on top of each avocado half some finely chopped
   cilantro. Serve.

# Melon with Yogurt and Fresh Mint

3 small ripe melons
4 tablespoons lemon juice
One 16-ounce container low-fat
    plain yogurt

Salt and freshly ground black
    pepper to taste
A few fresh mint leaves, finely
    chopped and minced

6 SERVINGS

1. Slice each melon in two equal parts. Clean the insides and discard the seeds. Sprinkle some lemon juice over each half.
2. Place the yogurt in a bowl, add the remaining lemon juice, salt, pepper, and part of the finely chopped mint and mix well. Refrigerate until chilled.
3. Just before serving, fill each melon hollow with the yogurt mixture. Sprinkle the remaining chopped mint on the top of each melon. Serve it cold.

NOTE: This is particularly appetizing and refreshing during the hot weather months.

# Montpellier Dip

2 shallots (or 1 medium-size onion), chopped and minced
10 spinach leaves
10 branches of watercress
5 branches of chervil
5 branches of parsley
A few tarragon leaves
5 chive leaves, finely chopped

12 capers
1 small cucumber pickle (cornichon)
2 small garlic cloves
1 hard-boiled egg, crumbled
One 16-ounce container low-fat sour cream
2 tablespoons virgin olive oil

1. Place the shallots, spinach, watercress, chervil, parsley, and tarragon in a casserole. Add water to cover and boil for exactly 1 minute. Drain and then run cold water over the whole. Drain again and set aside.

2. Place the above ingredients in a food processor. Add the chives, capers, cucumber, and garlic cloves. Blend thoroughly.

3. Place the blended ingredients in a deep bowl. Add the crumbled hard-boiled egg, sour cream, and olive oil. Blend well all the ingredients with a fork. Place the mixture in the refrigerator until ready to use. Serve cold.

NOTE: This delicious dip can be used in many creative ways. Spread it over baguette slices or crackers. Use it to fill the center of hard-boiled eggs. Or use it as a dip with fresh vegetables such as broccoli, cauliflower, carrots, celery, etc.

# Warm Antipasto (Salad Tiède)

2 large red peppers
2 large yellow peppers
2 medium-size zucchini, sliced in
    half lengthwise
2 medium-size Vidalia onions,
    sliced in half lengthwise

4 medium-size ripe tomatoes, sliced
    in round halves
16 pitted black olives
8 pitted green olives
4 teaspoons capers

## Vinaigrette

¼ cup extra-virgin olive oil
A dash of salt
4 tablespoons wine vinegar

Freshly ground black pepper
1 tablespoon finely chopped fresh
    marjoram, as garnish

4 SERVINGS

1. Preheat the broiler. Trim the peppers and cut them in perfect halves lengthwise. Place them under the broiler, turning them often, until the skin becomes black and blistered. Remove them from the oven, place them in a paper bag for about 10–15 minutes, and then strip off the skin. Discard the skin, the stems, and the seeds. Place the peppers on an ovenproof plate and set them aside.

2. Preheat the oven to 350°. Oil thoroughly a long baking dish and place the zucchini, onions, tomatoes, all the olives, and the capers on the dish. Brush the tops of the vegetables with olive oil and sprinkle on a dash of salt. Place in the oven for about 20 minutes. During the last 5 minutes also place in the oven the plate of peppers.

3. While the vegetables are in the oven prepare the vinaigrette by mixing well the ¼ cup oil, vinegar, salt, and pepper. Whisk it until all the elements are well blended.

4. After 20 minutes, just before serving, remove the vegetables from the oven. Arrange decoratively in each of four serving dishes: 1 red

pepper half, 1 yellow pepper half, 1 zucchini half, 1 onion half, and 2 tomato halves. Place 4 black olives and 2 green olives on each plate. Sprinkle 1 teaspoon capers on each plate. Pour the vinaigrette equally over the four portions. Top each serving with finely chopped marjoram. Serve immediately, warm or at least at room temperature.

# Goat Cheese and Fresh Herbs Dip

12 ounces fresh goat cheese

8 tablespoons extra-virgin olive oil

1/2 cup low-fat sour cream (or plain yogurt)

2 teaspoons minced fresh thyme

2 teaspoons finely chopped fresh rosemary

3 tablespoons finely chopped fresh parsley

3 tablespoons finely chopped fresh chives

1 teaspoon finely chopped fresh oregano

1 garlic clove, finely minced

1/2 teaspoon french mustard

Salt and freshly ground black pepper to taste

MAKES 1 SMALL BOWL

1. Place the cheese, oil, and sour cream in a blender or food processor. Whirl and mix well.

2. Place the cheese mixture in a deep serving bowl. Add all the herbs, garlic, mustard, salt, and pepper. Whisk and blend all the ingredients well with a fork. Refrigerate the dip for several hours.

NOTE: Serve the dip with baguette slices or crackers, or use it with fresh vegetables from the garden. It is delicious over tomato slices!

# Asparagus-Roasted Pepper Canapés

½ pound fresh thin asparagus
One 8-ounce jar roasted peppers
6 slices whole wheat bread
French mustard, as needed

6 slices Swiss Emmental cheese
  (or other)
Capers, as needed

24 CANAPÉS

1. Preheat the oven to 300°. Boil the asparagus in salted water to cover for 2 minutes. Drain them thoroughly. Slice them into pieces 2 inches long and set aside.
2. Drain the peppers and slice them into thin pieces about 2 inches long.
3. Trim off the crust from the bread slices and spread a bit of mustard over each slice. Cut each slice in four equal parts.
4. Cut each cheese slice in four equal parts and place each piece on the top of the corresponding bread piece.
5. Butter thoroughly a long ovenproof serving dish and place the small bread slices into it. Arrange 3 asparagus pieces on each bread slice, 2 at the edges and 1 at the center. In between them place 2 thin red pepper pieces. At the center of the canapé, on both sides of the asparagus in the center, place 2 capers.
6. Place the canapés in the oven for about 8–10 minutes. Remove them from the oven and serve them warm.

# Tapenade Provençale

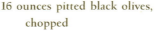

16 ounces pitted black olives, chopped
6 ounces capers
4 garlic cloves, peeled
2 tablespoons lemon juice
3 tablespoons herbs de Provence (thyme, basil, bay leaf, rosemary)

Freshly ground black pepper to taste
A few sprigs of fresh parsley, finely chopped
3/4 cup extra-virgin olive oil

ABOUT 1½ CUPS

Place all the above ingredients except the olive oil in a food processor or a blender. Add the olive oil gradually as the ingredients blend, until the mixture turns into a smooth paste. Taste for seasonings and adjust them as needed. For example, add a bit more lemon juice or herbs de Provence, if necessary. Refrigerate until ready to be used.

NOTE: This wonderful creamy Provençale concoction can be served with aperitifs over slices of fresh country bread, french baguette slices, or water crackers. I occasionally mix the tapenade with egg yolk to fill hard-boiled eggs.

# Eggplant Terrine (Terrine d'Aubergines)

Tomato Sauce (page 166)
7 tablespoons extra-virgin olive oil
1 pound eggplants, cut in chunks
4 red peppers, seeded and diced
3 medium-size onions, coarsely
    chopped
4 garlic cloves, minced

4 eggs
6 slices whole wheat bread,
    crumbled
3 tablespoons dried herbs (basil,
    thyme, and rosemary)
Salt and freshly ground black
    pepper to taste

6 SERVINGS

1. Pour the oil into a good-size, nonstick skillet, add the vegetables including the garlic, and sauté over low-medium heat for about 10 minutes. Stir frequently. When the vegetables are done, crush them thoroughly with a masher, and set them aside.

2. Preheat the oven to 350°. In a deep bowl beat the eggs thoroughly and add the bread crumbs, herbs, salt, and pepper and blend the ingredients well.

3. Mix and blend well the reserved vegetables and egg mixture. Butter generously a bread mold or pan and place the vegetable and egg mixture in it.

4. Place the bread mold in the oven. Cook for about 25–30 minutes. When the dish is done, unmold it carefully onto a serving plate. Allow to cool.

5. Carefully cut the eggplant bread into 6 slices, and place them into serving plates. Pour some of the previously prepared tomato sauce over each slice. Serve immediately.

   NOTE: This dish is an excellent appetizer. It can be presented hot or cold at the table. During the summer months, refrigerate it and then serve it cold. (The sauce in that case should be served cold.)

# Spicy Black Bean Dip

1 medium-size onion, chopped
One 16-ounce can black beans,
    drained
3 garlic cloves, minced
1 green bell pepper, sliced and
    diced
1/3 cup chopped fresh cilantro

3 tablespoons lemon juice (or lime)
1 small jalapeño pepper, seeded and
    diced
1 tablespoon cumin
Salt to taste
One 8-ounce container low-fat sour
    cream

ABOUT 2 CUPS

1. Place all the above ingredients, except the sour cream, in a food processor. Blend well and place the mixture in a deep bowl.

2. Add the sour cream to the mixture, and with the help of a fork, blend thoroughly all the ingredients. Place the bowl in the refrigerator until the dip is ready to be served. Serve cold with tortilla chips. It is enough for about 10 to 12 people.

SOUPS

# Spicy Lentil Soup

2½ cups black lentils
½ cup long-grain rice
¼ cup olive oil
4 onions, finely chopped
1 celery stalk, thinly sliced
1 large carrot, peeled and cut into
    small dice
2 tomatoes, peeled and diced
3 tablespoons tomato paste

4 garlic cloves, minced
11 cups vegetable stock (or water)
Salt and cayenne pepper to taste
2 teaspoons paprika
1 long lemon peel
1 tablespoon cumin
Plain yogurt, as garnish
Finely chopped fresh cilantro, as
    garnish

6-8 SERVINGS

1. Place the lentils and rice in a container filled with water for 30 minutes. Rinse and drain them.

2. Heat the oil to low-medium in a large soup pot, and then add the onions, celery, carrot, and tomatoes, and sauté lightly over medium heat, while stirring continually. After 4 or 5 minutes add the tomato paste and the garlic. Continue stirring for another minute or two.

3. Add the vegetable stock or water, lentils and rice, salt and cayenne pepper, paprika, lemon peel, and cumin. Stir well. Cover the pot and bring the soup to a boil. Allow it to boil for about 5 minutes.

4. Reduce the heat to low-medium, stir the soup, re-cover the pot, and allow the soup to simmer for 40–45 minutes, until the vegetables are thoroughly cooked. Check the seasonings and remove the lemon peel. Place 1 tablespoon plain yogurt at the center of each serving, surrounded by finely chopped cilantro. Serve the soup hot.

# Spring Spinach Soup

1 pound fresh spinach
4 tablespoons olive oil
1 large onion, finely chopped
2 tablespoons cornstarch
6½ cups vegetable stock (or water)
2 tablespoons lemon juice
One 8-ounce container low-fat sour
   cream

Salt and freshly ground black
   pepper to taste
A dash of nutmeg
Finely chopped fresh chervil, as
   garnish

4–6 SERVINGS

1. Wash and rinse the spinach well. Drain it thoroughly and chop it coarsely.
2. Heat the oil to low-medium in a soup pot and sauté the onion. Cook over low-medium heat, while stirring continually, for about 2 to 3 minutes.
3. Dilute the cornstarch in 1 cup vegetable stock or water, and add it gradually to the onion. Add the remaining stock or water and the lemon juice and bring the stock to a boil. Add the spinach and reduce the heat to low-medium. Cover the pot and simmer gently for 20 minutes. Allow the soup to cool for a few minutes, then add the remaining ingredients, except the chervil, and stir well.
4. Blend the soup in a blender or food processor. Pour the soup back into the pot and reheat it if you are planning to serve it hot. Otherwise, place it in the refrigerator for several hours and serve it chilled. Sprinkle finely chopped chervil on the top of the soup before serving.

NOTE: This is an ideal soup to serve in late spring, hence the name, or in early summer, when spinach is in season and it can be freshly harvested from the garden or purchased at a farmers' market.

# Candlemas Black-Eyed Pea Soup

8 tablespoons good cooking oil (or olive oil)

2 leeks, thinly sliced (including the green parts)

1 large onion, chopped

4 carrots, peeled and diced

2 potatoes, peeled and cubed

2 cups dried black-eyed peas

12 cups water

1 bay leaf

Salt and freshly ground black pepper to taste

A pinch of cumin

1/3 cup minced fresh cilantro (or parsley), plus more (finely chopped) as garnish

6-8 SERVINGS

1. Pour the oil into a soup kettle and, over low-medium heat, sauté the leeks and the onion for about 3 minutes.

2. Add the carrots, potatoes, the black-eyed peas, water, bay leaf, salt, pepper, and cumin. Bring the soup to a boil, then reduce the heat to low-medium. Cover the kettle, and cook the soup slowly for 1 hour, or until the peas are cooked. Stir from time to time, so the soup does not stick at the bottom.

3. When the soup is done, remove the bay leaf. Allow the soup to cool for a while, and then blend it in a blender or food processor until it achieves a smooth, creamy consistency. Reheat the soup, add the 1/3 cup minced cilantro, and stir well. Check the seasonings, including the cumin. Do not let the soup come to a second boil. Serve the soup hot, with finely chopped cilantro as garnish.

NOTE: This soup takes its name from the feast of the Presentation of the Lord in the Temple, celebrated annually on February 2 by the churches of the East and West. This feast is commonly known in English as Candlemas, for candles play an important role in the day's liturgy. The theme of light permeates the entire celebration of the feast, evocative of the words of the elder Simeon, who called the Christ Child "a light to enlighten the nations." The candles are blessed at the beginning of the rite, and then carried by the faithful in the procession that follows, and later placed in front of the icon of the feast, where they represent the silent petitions of our prayers.

# Creamy Sorrel and Lettuce Potage

4 tablespoons butter or margarine
6 cups thinly shredded sorrel leaves
1 medium head Boston lettuce,
    thinly shredded
1 medium-size onion, finely
    chopped
2 garlic cloves, minced
4 cups water

Salt and freshly ground black
    pepper to taste
A pinch of dried thyme
2 eggs
2 cups milk (for a richer version of
    the soup you may use half-
    and-half)
Croutons, as garnish

6 SERVINGS

1. Melt the butter in a soup pot and add the shredded sorrel, shredded lettuce, chopped onion, and minced garlic. Cook over low heat until the ingredients gradually wilt and turn saucy. Stir constantly.
2. Add the water, salt, pepper, and thyme. Stir the ingredients well and cover the pot. Bring the soup to a boil and then lower the heat to low-medium. Cook for about 20 minutes.
3. In a blender mix well the eggs with the milk. Pour this mixture into the soup and mix it well. Continue cooking and stirring, but do not let the soup reach the boiling point. Serve hot, topping each serving with croutons.

# Potage Condé

2 cups dried red beans (or two
    16-ounce cans kidney beans,
    drained)
2 large carrots, peeled and cubed
2 onions, chopped
2 garlic cloves, chopped and minced

9 cups water
1 bouquet garni (a branch of thyme,
    rosemary, and bay leaf tied up
    with fine thread)
Salt and freshly ground black
    pepper to taste

6 SERVINGS

1. Soak the dried beans overnight. Drain them and place them in a soup kettle. Add the carrots, onions, garlic, water, and bouquet garni.
2. Bring the water to a boil, then cover the pot, and lower the heat to low-medium. Cook for about 1 hour, stirring from time to time and adding more water if necessary.
3. After 1 hour, check to see if the beans are well cooked. Add the salt and pepper. Stir thoroughly, remove the bouquet garni, turn off the heat, and re-cover the pot until it cools.
4. Blend the soup in a blender or food processor until it achieves an even, creamy consistency. Reheat the soup and serve it hot.

# Monastery Harvest Soup

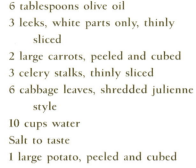

IT IS ONLY WITH THE HEART THAT ONE

CAN SEE RIGHTLY; WHAT IS ESSENTIAL IS

INVISIBLE TO THE EYE.

ANTOINE DE SAINT-EXUPÉRY

6 tablespoons olive oil
3 leeks, white parts only, thinly
    sliced
2 large carrots, peeled and cubed
3 celery stalks, thinly sliced
6 cabbage leaves, shredded julienne
    style
10 cups water
Salt to taste
1 large potato, peeled and cubed

1 turnip, washed and cubed
1 cup thinly sliced (about 1 inch
    long) string beans
1 cup green peas (fresh or frozen)
Freshly ground black pepper to
    taste
1 long french bread (baguette)
Cheddar cheese, grated as needed
Finely chopped fresh parsley, as
    garnish

6-8 SERVINGS

1. Pour the oil into a good-size nonstick soup pot. Add the leeks and
   sauté briefly over low-medium heat for about 2 or 3 minutes. Add the
   carrots, celery, and shredded cabbage, and continue cooking for another minute or two, stirring all the while.
2. Add the water and salt. Bring the soup to a quick boil, then lower the
   heat to medium, cover the pot, and continue cooking for about 15
   minutes. Add the potato, turnip, string beans, peas, and pepper.
   Lower the heat to low-medium, stir the soup, cover the pot, and simmer for 30 minutes.
3. Just before the soup is done, preheat the oven to 350°. Slice the
   baguette, place the slices on a baking sheet, and sprinkle some of the
   grated cheese on top of each slice. Bake for about 5 minutes.
4. When the soup is done, check the seasonings. Serve the soup hot and
   sprinkle some finely chopped parsley on each serving. Place the bread
   on a serving plate and pass it around.

NOTE: This is a typical soup served at the monastery during the period of the harvest. Since we are blessed to have a good *potager*—that is, a kitchen garden—we avail ourselves of the variety of products from the garden to make this soup. Sometimes we change a vegetable or two, depending on what the garden is producing at that time.

# Grandmother's Bread and Garlic Soup

½ cup extra-virgin olive oil
16 garlic cloves, peeled and coarsely
 chopped
6 slices stale bread
6 cups vegetable broth (or water)
3 vegetable bouillon cubes (if water
 is used)
5 tablespoons tomato paste

1 tablespoon paprika
1 teaspoon cumin
Salt to taste
A pinch of cayenne
6 eggs
A bunch of fresh parsley, finely
 chopped, as garnish

6 SERVINGS

1. Pour the oil into a nonstick casserole or soup pot. Sauté the garlic in the oil over medium heat for about 1 minute, Do not let it turn brown. Remove and set the garlic aside. Leave the oil in the pot.
2. Fry the bread slices on both sides in the same garlic-flavored oil. Remove the bread and set the slices aside.
3. Pour the vegetable broth (or the water and bouillon cubes) into the casserole, over the remaining oil. Add the tomato paste, paprika, cumin, salt, cayenne, and the reserved cooked garlic. Bring the soup to a boil. Reduce the heat to low-medium and simmer for 20 minutes. Cover the casserole.
4. During the last 5 minutes of simmering, break the eggs into the soup and poach them. Place 1 bread slice on each soup plate, pour some of the soup on top, and put 1 egg on top of each slice. Sprinkle some of the parsley over the top of each egg before serving. Serve hot.

# Tourangelle Soup

4 tablespoons (½ stick) butter
4 leeks, white parts only, sliced
2 medium-size turnips, cubed
8 cups water (or vegetable stock)
2 potatoes, cubed

1 cup fresh peas (or frozen)
6 white cabbage leaves, cut into
   small pieces
Salt and freshly ground black
   pepper to taste

6 SERVINGS

1. Melt the butter in a soup pot. Add the leeks and the turnips and sauté them lightly over low-medium heat for several minutes. Stir frequently.

2. Add 8 cups water or vegetable stock and the potatoes, and bring to a boil. Lower the heat to simmer, cover the pot, and let the soup cook gently for about 50 minutes. Stir occasionally.

3. After the 50 minutes, add the peas, cabbage leaves, salt, and pepper. Stir. Re-cover the pot and continue simmering for another 50 minutes. Serve the soup hot.

# Easy Couscous Soup

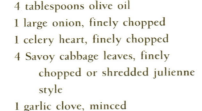

4 tablespoons olive oil
1 large onion, finely chopped
1 celery heart, finely chopped
4 Savoy cabbage leaves, finely
 chopped or shredded julienne
 style
1 garlic clove, minced
1 cup couscous

8$\frac{1}{2}$ cups water (or vegetable stock)
1 vegetable bouillon cube (if water
 is used)
1 bay leaf
1 tablespoon tamari sauce
Salt and freshly ground black
 pepper to taste
Fresh thyme leaves, as garnish

6-8 SERVINGS

1. Pour the oil into a soup kettle, add the onion, celery, cabbage, and garlic. Sauté lightly over low-medium heat for about 3 minutes, stirring often.
2. Add the couscous, and mix well. Add the water and bouillon cube (or the vegetable stock), bay leaf, tamari sauce, salt, and pepper and bring the soup to a boil. Stir well, lower the heat to low, cover the pot, and allow the soup to simmer for 1 hour.
3. Remove the bay leaf, check the seasonings, and serve the soup hot, sprinkling some fresh thyme leaves on the top of each serving.

# Hearty Chickpea Soup

One 15-ounce can chickpeas,
    drained (or 1 cup cooked and
    drained)
2 onions, finely chopped
2 medium carrots, peeled and
    cubed
1 bay leaf
8 cups water
1/4 cup olive oil

4 garlic cloves, minced
3 tomatoes, peeled and coarsely
    chopped
2 cups finely chopped spinach
Salt and freshly ground black
    pepper
1/2 teaspoon paprika
Finely chopped fresh parsley, as
    garnish

6 SERVINGS

1. Place the chickpeas, onions, carrots, and bay leaf in a large soup kettle. Add 7 cups of the water. Over medium heat bring the water to a boil. Simmer for 20 minutes over low heat.

2. Heat the oil in a separate saucepan. Add the garlic and tomatoes. Sauté for about 4–5 minutes over medium heat until the mixture becomes saucy.

3. Add the tomato sauce to the soup. Add the spinach, salt, pepper, and paprika. Add the remaining cup water and again bring the soup to a boil. Re-cover the pot and simmer the soup over low-medium heat for 20 minutes. Discard the bay leaf. Serve the soup hot, with some of the finely chopped parsley sprinkled over each serving.

EGG DISHES

# Rocamadour Cheese Puff

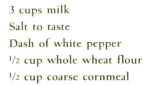

3 cups milk
Salt to taste
Dash of white pepper
½ cup whole wheat flour
½ cup coarse cornmeal

5 ounces New York or Vermont
    Cheddar cheese, grated
5 eggs, separated
⅓ cup grated Gruyère cheese (or
    mozzarella)

4-6 SERVINGS

1. Preheat the oven to 400°. Pour the milk into a large saucepan. Add the salt and white pepper. Heat the milk over low-medium heat. Add the whole wheat flour gradually, whisking steadily. Add the cornmeal and continue whisking steadily.
2. Continue cooking until the mixture achieves a thick, smooth consistency. At this point, add the grated Cheddar cheese and mix well. Remove the saucepan from the heat and allow the mixture to cool.
3. Beat the egg yolks and add them to the mixture. Add the Gruyère ( or mozzarella) and stir well until the ingredients are thoroughly blended.
4. Butter thoroughly a soufflé dish or another ovenproof dish. Pour the mixture into it. Beat the egg whites stiff and fold gradually into the mixture.
5. Place the dish into the oven. Lower the temperature to 350° and bake for about 25–30 minutes, until the top turns golden brown. Serve immediately.

# St. Benedict's Omelet

2 ounces goat cheese
2 tablespoons finely chopped fresh
    parsley
2 tablespoons finely chopped fresh
    chives
2 tablespoons finely chopped fresh
    chervil

5 eggs
Salt and freshly ground black
    pepper to taste
Butter, as needed

2 SERVINGS

1. Combine the cheese and the herbs in a bowl. Mash and mix them well with the help of a fork. Make sure the ingredients are well blended.
2. In a separate bowl beat the eggs lightly, add the salt and pepper, and beat some more.
3. Melt the butter in a nonstick omelet or crepe pan over medium heat. Tilt the pan around until the butter covers the whole surface. Pour the egg mixture into it and tilt again until the mixture covers the entire surface. Cook for about 4–5 minutes.
4. When the eggs are cooked, place the cheese-herb mixture in the center of the omelet. Spread it with a spatula. Roll the omelet over the filling and enclose it gently. Slice the omelet in two perfect halves and serve immediately.

# Potato Omelet Basque Style

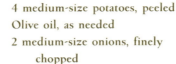

4 medium-size potatoes, peeled
Olive oil, as needed
2 medium-size onions, finely
  chopped

2 bell peppers, finely chopped
8 eggs (2 per person)
Salt and freshly ground black
  pepper to taste

4 SERVINGS

1. Slice the potatoes in very small cubes. Heat some olive oil in a large skillet and sauté the potatoes over low-medium heat.
2. When the potatoes are half-cooked, add the onions and bell peppers, and continue cooking while stirring continually. When the vegetables are cooked, remove them from the skillet, and set them aside. (Keep them warm.)
3. Beat the 4 of the eggs in a deep bowl, add the salt and pepper, and beat some more. Pour some olive oil on the skillet and raise the heat to medium. When the oil is very hot, pour the egg mixture into the skillet. Spread the eggs evenly with a spatula. When the egg mixture sets firmly on the bottom, place half the potato mixture in the center. Gently fold one half of the omelet over the other half. Slice the omelet in half and serve immediately on hot plates.
4. Repeat step 3 with the remaining eggs and potato mixture.

NOTE: This recipe can also be used for making 4 individual omelets by dividing the eggs and potato portions equally in four parts.

# Scrambled Eggs Navarra Style

( Oeufs Brouillés Navarrais )

14 tablespoons olive oil

3 potatoes, peeled and cubed

Salt to taste

3 tomatoes, peeled and coarsely chopped

2 onions, chopped

2 medium-size zucchini, diced

2 bell peppers, finely chopped

3 garlic cloves, minced

8 eggs

1/2 cup milk

Freshly ground black pepper to taste

4-6 SERVINGS

1. Heat 6 tablespoons of the oil in a medium-size frying pan, add the potatoes, and sauté them over low-medium heat. Sprinkle some salt over the potatoes, and stir occasionally. When the potatoes are done, turn off the heat, cover the pan, and keep them warm.

2. Heat the remaining 8 tablespoons oil (add more if necessary) in a large separate frying pan, and sauté the remaining vegetables and garlic over low-medium heat. Sprinkle a dash of salt over the vegetables and stir frequently.

3. In a large bowl beat the eggs well, add the milk, salt, and pepper, and beat slowly with a mixer or by hand.

4. Add the potatoes to the rest of the vegetables and carefully mix them evenly. Pour the egg-milk mixture over the vegetables and cook over medium heat, stirring often. When the eggs begin to set, remove the pan from the heat and serve immediately, while the eggs are still moist.

NOTE: Very often this dish is served in the Basque country on the top of a toasted slice of bread. Either way, this is an appetizing dish for a Sunday brunch or light lunch.

# Asparagus Frittata

8 tablespoons olive oil

4 medium-size potatoes, peeled and thinly sliced

6 scallions, coarsely chopped

10 fresh asparagus stalks, washed and drained

2 tablespoons finely chopped fresh parsley

Salt and freshly ground black pepper to taste

3 egg whites

5 whole eggs

4 SERVINGS

1. Pour the oil into a nonstick skillet, and sauté the potatoes and scallions over low-medium heat for several minutes. Stir and turn them over occasionally. (Don't overcook!)

2. Trim the asparagus and slice the stalks into 1/2-inch pieces. Boil them in salted water to cover for exactly 2 minutes. Drain them thoroughly and add them to the potato-scallion mixture. Mix them well and cook for an extra minute. Sprinkle on the parsley, salt, and pepper and mix again.

3. Whisk the egg whites in a bowl. Whisk the whole eggs in a larger bowl, add the egg whites, a dash of salt and pepper, and mix the ingredients well. Pour the egg mixture over the vegetables in the skillet. When the eggs firm up, with the help of a large flat plate, turn the frittata over onto the plate. Slide the frittata back into the skillet and cook the other side for about a minute. Slice the frittata in four even slices and serve immediately.

LOVE RULES WITHOUT A SWORD,

AND BINDS WITHOUT A CORD.

ANCIENT EGYPTIAN PROVERB

# St. Joseph's Frittata

4 tablespoons (½ stick) butter
1 onion, coarsely chopped
1 carrot, peeled and finely grated
1 potato, peeled and thinly sliced
1 zucchini, thinly sliced
1 large tomato, coarsely chopped

7 eggs
½ cup heavy cream
Salt and pepper to taste
A handful of fresh parsley, finely
    chopped
¼ cup grated Parmesan cheese

4 SERVINGS

1. Preheat the oven to 300°. Melt 2 tablespoons of the butter in a large cast-iron skillet. Add the onion, carrot, potato, zucchini, and tomato. Sauté the vegetables over medium heat until they are cooked, turning the potato and the zucchini over occasionally.

2. Beat the eggs in a deep bowl, add the heavy cream, salt and pepper, parsley, and cheese and beat some more until all ingredients are well blended. Add the vegetables and again blend all the elements well.

3. Clean the skillet and dry it thoroughly. Melt the remaining 2 tablespoons butter in the skillet and run it over the whole skillet bottom. When hot, pour the egg-vegetable mixture into it and cook over low-medium heat until the bottom part seems well cooked. Check with a spatula. Remove the skillet from the heat, place it in the oven, and bake until the top part is evenly cooked and solid. Remove from the oven, slice in four equal portions, and serve hot.

# Matafam

4 shallots
7 eggs
1½ cups milk
4 ounces flour (preferably whole
   wheat)

Salt and freshly ground black
   pepper to taste
2 ounces (½ stick) butter

4 SERVINGS

1. Chop the shallots finely.
2. In a deep bowl beat the eggs. Add the milk and beat some more using, if possible, an electric mixer. Add the flour, salt, and pepper and mix some more, until the ingredients are well blended. Add the shallots and mix by hand. Let the mixture rest for 30 minutes.
3. Preheat the oven to 350°. Melt the butter in a large cast-iron skillet. Pour the egg mixture into it and cook over medium heat. When the bottom begins to set, remove the skillet from the heat, and place it in the oven for 15–20 minutes, until the matafam is done. Serve hot.

NOTE: The name of this peasant country dish, which means "kill the hunger," "*tué la faim*," or in Spanish "*mata el hambre*," comes from the Besançon region of France, an area that was occupied for a long time by Spanish troops during early centuries. Hence the origin of the name.

# Omelette Mère Poulard

6 eggs, separated
1 tablespoon water
Salt and freshly ground black
    pepper to taste

2 tablespoons heavy cream
3 tablespoons butter

2 SERVINGS

1. Place the egg yolks in a deep bowl. Add the water, salt, and pepper and beat thoroughly with a whisk or mixer.
2. In a separate bowl place the egg whites, heavy cream, and a dash of salt and pepper. Beat stiff with the help of a whisk or mixer.
3. Melt the butter over medium heat in a good-size skillet. When the skillet is well heated pour the egg yolk mixture into the skillet and let it run throughout the whole surface. When it begins to set, pour the egg white mixture over it, and spread evenly with a spatula. Cover the skillet for 1 minute, and immediately, carefully fold half the omelet over the other half. Continue cooking for 1/2 minute over low-medium heat. Cut the omelet in two, and serve on hot plates.

NOTE: This omelet, famous all over the world because of its association with Mont St. Michel, was the creation of a certain Mme. Poulard, who passed on her secret recipe to her son. The secret consists in moving the skillet constantly while the omelet is being made, and of course, to be sure to separate the egg yolks and the whites.

# Eggs Cocotte in Pesto Sauce

## (OEUFS COCOTTE AU PISTOU)

20 fresh basil leaves
4 teaspoons pignoli nuts
5 tablespoons olive oil
1 garlic clove, peeled
1½ pints heavy cream
6 eggs

Salt and freshly ground black
    pepper to taste
A pinch of nutmeg
12 teaspoons grated Parmesan
    cheese

6 SERVINGS

1. Preheat the oven to 300°. Butter thoroughly 6 ramekins (small French porcelain bowls). Prepare the pesto sauce by mixing the basil, pignoli, olive oil, and garlic in a food processor. Mix well and then pour the sauce into a bowl. Add the heavy cream and blend the ingredients well by hand. Refrigerate the sauce until ready to use.

2. Cover the bottom of each prepared ramekin with a bit of the pesto sauce. Break an egg in the center of each ramekin. Sprinkle some salt, pepper, and a pinch of nutmeg on the top of each egg. Cover the eggs with the rest of the creamy pesto sauce. Sprinkle 2 teaspoons Parmesan cheese over the top surface of each egg.

3. Put the ramekins into a pan large enough to hold them. Carefully pour some water into the pan, about 2 inches high. Avoid getting water into the ramekins. Bake the ramekins in the bain-marie for about 10 minutes maximum. When the eggs are ready, serve them immediately, accompanied by fresh french bread on the side.

# Eggs in Potato Croustades

4 good-size Idaho potatoes
4 tablespoons butter
4 tablespoons milk
Salt and freshly ground black
    pepper to taste

4 tablespoons finely chopped fresh
    parsley
4 eggs

4 SERVINGS

1. Preheat the oven to 350°. Bake the potatoes for 50–60 minutes, until tender. Cut a thin slice off the top of the potato. Scoop out carefully the inside of the potatoes, leaving a $^1/_4$-inch shell intact.

2. In a bowl, mash the scooped-out parts of the potatoes. Add the butter, milk, salt, pepper, and parsley and mix well. Place about half of this mixture back into the potatoes leaving a hollow space for the eggs.

3. Break an egg at the center of each potato and season it with salt and pepper. Use the remaining potato mixture to build a decorative edge on the top of the shell and around the egg. Place the potatoes in a well-buttered ovenproof dish and bake for about 15 minutes. When the eggs are set the dish is done. Serve hot.

NOTE: This is an excellent dish for a Sunday brunch, a welcome variety from the usual egg dishes served on those occasions.

# Spinach Soufflé

1 pound spinach (fresh or frozen),
    coarsely chopped
1 onion, coarsely chopped
Vegetable oil, as needed (about 3
    tablespoons)
5 eggs, separated
1 1/2 cups White Sauce (page 159)

1/2 cup heavy cream
Salt and freshly ground pepper to
    taste, if needed
5 tablespoons grated Parmesan or
    Romano cheese, plus more for
    the soufflé dish

4-6 SERVINGS

1. Boil the spinach over medium heat for 20 minutes, then drain it thoroughly. Squeeze every bit of water out of it. Set aside.

2. Preheat the oven to 350°. Place the onion in a large skillet, add the oil, and sauté over low-medium heat for 3–4 minutes. Add the reserved spinach, and continue sautéing for another 5 minutes. Blend the ingredients well. Turn off the heat and let the mixture rest.

3. In a deep bowl beat the eggs yolks with a mixer. Add the white sauce and continue blending with the mixer. Add the heavy cream, salt and pepper if needed (white sauce already contains both), and the 5 tablespoons grated cheese, and continue blending with the mixer. Add the spinach-onion mixture, and blend all the ingredients thoroughly with a fork.

4. In a separate bowl beat the egg whites with a mixer until stiff. Fold the stiffly beaten egg whites slowly into the spinach mixture.

5. Butter thoroughly an ovenproof soufflé dish and then sprinkle some grated cheese over the butter. Carefully pour the mixture into the dish. Bake for 25–30 minutes. When the soufflé is done, serve immediately.

# Asparagus Soufflé

24 asparagus spears
3 shallots (or 1 onion), finely
    chopped
Oil, as needed (about 3
    tablespoons)
2 cups White Sauce (page 159)
6 eggs, separated

Salt and freshly ground black
    pepper to taste
12 tablespoons grated Gruyère
    cheese (or other cheese, such
    as Cheddar or Parmesan), plus
    more for the soufflé dish

6 SERVINGS

1. Trim the asparagus, discarding the tough parts. Chop the rest into pieces 2 inches long and boil them in salted water for about 10 minutes, until tender. Drain them thoroughly.
2. Preheat the oven to 350°. Place the shallots in a good-size skillet, add the oil, and sauté over low-medium heat for about 3 minutes. Add the asparagus and continue sautéing for another 3 minutes. STIR continually. Blend the asparagus mixture in a food processor. Set it aside.
3. In a deep bowl beat the egg yolks. Use an electric mixer if possible. Add the white sauce and continue blending with the mixer. Add the salt and pepper (only if needed, the white sauce is already seasoned), and 6 tablespoons grated cheese. Mix some more, then add the asparagus puree and 6 tablespoons more of grated cheese, and blend the ingredients thoroughly with a fork.
4. In a separate bowl beat the egg whites until stiff. Fold the stiffly beaten egg whites slowly into the asparagus puree.
5. Butter thoroughly a good-size ovenproof soufflé dish and sprinkle some grated cheese over the butter. Pour the asparagus puree into the dish. Bake for about 30 minutes. When the soufflé is done, serve immediately.

# Trucchia

1/2 pound Swiss chard, green parts only
1 onion
About 12 tablespoons olive oil

6 eggs
1/2 cup grated Parmesan cheese
Salt and freshly ground black pepper to taste

4-6 SERVINGS

1. Wash well the Swiss chard leaves, and then chop them finely. Chop the onion.

2. Pour 6 tablespoons of the olive oil into a large nonstick skillet, and place it over medium heat. When the oil is hot, add the chard and the onion. Cover the skillet and cook for about 2 minutes. Then lower the heat to low, stir well, re-cover the skillet, and continue cooking for another 4 minutes or so until the chard wilts and is thoroughly cooked.

3. In a deep bowl beat the eggs. Add the cheese, salt, and pepper, and beat some more. Add the chard-onion mixture and blend well.

4. Pour the remaining 6 tablespoons oil into a large, clean, nonstick skillet, and place it over medium heat. When the oil is hot, pour the egg mixture into it. Cover the skillet and cook for about 2–3 minutes. When the bottom part is cooked, with a spatula carefully slide the trucchia onto a large plate, and then return it to the skillet upside down. Continue cooking until the lower part is done. Cut in four or six even slices and serve. It can also be cut into small squares and served at room temperature with an aperitif.

CREPES AND PANCAKES

# Mussel Crepes

THERE IS AN AMAZING THING THAT
HAPPENS WHEN YOU BEGIN TO
SIMPLIFY YOUR LIFE: A LOT OF THOSE
ONCE VALUED BUT RESTRICTING
BELIEFS . . . START TO HAVE LESS
INFLUENCE ON YOU. YOU BEGIN TO
REALIZE IT'S OKAY TO RELAX, AND
TO DO NOTHING, AND EVEN TO GO
TO BED EARLY JUST FOR THE EASE OF IT.

ELAINE ST. JAMES

4 pounds mussels
2/3 cup dry white wine
1 large leek, thinly sliced (white
      part only)

5 sprigs of parsley, finely chopped
7 black peppercorns, crushed

*Crepe Batter*

4 eggs
2 tablespoons olive oil
1¼ cups flour
A pinch of salt

3 cups milk
1–2 teaspoons cold water, if needed

Melted butter (or oil), as needed
½ cup heavy cream

6 SERVINGS

1. Wash the mussels and discard those that are open. (Pull off the beards.) Place the mussels in a good-size saucepan. Add the wine, leek, parsley, and peppercorns. Bring the liquid to a quick boil, then reduce the heat to low-medium, cover the saucepan tightly, and simmer for about 10–15 minutes. Stir occasionally, so the shells get to open. Discard the shells and those mussels that remain shut. Drain them and save the liquid. Refrigerate while making batter.

2. In a large, deep bowl mix the eggs, oil, flour, and salt and beat with a mixer, adding 1 cup of the milk at a time. The batter must reach the consistency of heavy cream and should be free of flour lumps. If the batter is too thick, add 1 or 2 teaspoons cold water and continue to mix until it is light and smooth. Refrigerate the batter for an hour or two.

3. Preheat the oven to 300°. Heat a 6- or 8-inch crepe skillet over high heat and lightly grease the entire skillet with a bit of melted butter (or oil if preferred), by using a small pastry brush (or by tilting the

pan over and over again until all the surface is greased). Using a small ladle pour the batter into the skillet. Tip it immediately so that the batter covers the entire bottom of the skillet and quickly becomes firm. Cook the crepe for about 1 minute, until it begins to show signs of turning brown around the rim. Turn it over rapidly with a spatula and cook the reverse side for another minute. When the crepe is done, slide it gently onto a flat plate. Brush the skillet once more with melted butter (or oil) and repeat the process until all the crepes are made (about 12).

4. Butter thoroughly a large baking dish. Fill each crepe with some of the mussel-leek mixture, roll them up, and place them carefully in the baking dish, one next to the other. When all the crepes are in the pan, mix the liquid saved from the cooking (what is left) with the heavy cream, and pour over the entire dish of crepes. Bake for about 20 minutes. Serve them hot, allowing 2 crepes per person.

# Crepes Camembert

4 eggs
2 tablespoons vegetable oil
1¼ cups flour (half whole wheat
    and half white flour)

A pinch of salt
3 cups milk
½ cup water
Oil (or melted butter), as needed

### Filling

3 tablespoons butter
½ pound mushrooms, thinly sliced
1 medium-size onion, thinly sliced
30 spinach leaves, chopped
Salt and freshly ground black
    pepper to taste

1 ounce Camembert, cut into thin
    slices
2 tablespoons heavy cream

### Topping

Heavy cream, as needed

6 SERVINGS

1. In a large, deep bowl, mix the eggs, oil, flour, and salt and whisk with a mixer. Keep whisking, adding 1 cup of milk at a time. Add the water and keep whisking until a batter consistency free of lumps is achieved. The batter should be light and smooth. Refrigerate the batter for 1 or 2 hours before using.

2. Preheat the oven to 300°. Heat a 6- or 8-inch crepe skillet over medium-high heat and using a pastry brush, lightly grease the entire surface with a bit of oil or melted butter. With a small ladle pour about 4 tablespoons of batter into the skillet and quickly swirl it around so it covers the bottom of the skillet. Cook the crepe for about 1 minute, until it begins to show signs of turning brown around the

rim. Flip the crepe or turn it over quickly with a spatula and cook the other side for 1–2 minutes. As the crepes are done, stack them on a plate. Brush the skillet with oil again and continue the process until all the crepes are made (about 12).

3. Melt the butter in a large nonstick skillet, and add the mushrooms and onion. Sauté gently over low-medium heat for about 3 minutes, stirring frequently. Add the spinach, salt, and pepper, and continue cooking for about 2 minutes until the spinach wilts. Add the Camembert and heavy cream. Toss and mix the ingredients. Remove the skillet from the heat.

4. Generously butter a long baking dish. Fill each crepe with the mushroom mixture, roll it up, and place it carefully in the dish, closely, one next to the other. When all the crepes are arranged in the dish, sprinkle heavy cream over the top and bake the crepes, uncovered, for about 15–20 minutes. Serve them hot, allowing 2 crepes per person.

# Ratatouille Crepes (Crêpes à la Ratatouille)

BEAUTY IS THE RADIANCE OF TRUTH,

THE FRAGRANCE OF GOODNESS.

VINCENT MCNABB

*Ratatouille*

4 tablespoons extra-virgin olive oil

2 large onions, coarsely chopped

2 medium-size eggplants, cubed

3 medium-size zucchini, cubed

2 pounds well-ripe tomatoes,
  seeded and coarsely chopped

1 sweet red pepper, seeded and cut
  into small pieces

3 garlic cloves, minced

3 sprigs of thyme

2 sprigs of rosemary

A few sage leaves, crushed

1 bay leaf

1/2 teaspoon paprika

Salt and freshly ground black
  pepper to taste

*Crepes Batter*

4 eggs

2 tablespoons olive oil

1 1/4 cups flour

A pinch of salt

3 cups milk

1–2 teaspoons cold water, if needed

Melted butter (or oil), as needed

1/2 cup heavy cream

6 SERVINGS

1. Heat the oil in a good-size cast-iron nonstick pot over medium heat. Add the onions, and sauté briefly for about 4 minutes, until they begin to turn golden. Add the eggplants and zucchini, and continue sautéing for another 4 minutes more or less. Add the tomatoes, pepper, garlic, thyme, rosemary, sage, bay leaf, paprika, salt, and pepper, and stir the ingredients several times. Reduce to low-medium heat, cover the pot, and continue cooking until the vegetables are tender and all the flavors have well blended. Stir from time to time. The cooking time should be approximately between 30 and 40 minutes. When the ratatouille is done, discard the thyme and rosemary sprigs and the bay leaf. Allow the ratatouille to cool a bit before filling the crepes. Refrigerate only if the ratatouille is not used within the next two hours.

2. In a large, deep bowl mix the eggs, oil, flour, and salt and beat with a mixer, adding 1 cup of milk at a time. The batter must reach the consistency of heavy cream and should be free of flour lumps. If the batter is too thick, add 1–2 teaspoons cold water and continue to mix until it is light and smooth. Refrigerate the batter for an hour or two before starting to use.

3. Preheat the oven to 300°. Heat a 6- or 8-inch crepe skillet over high heat and lightly grease the entire skillet with a bit of melted butter (or oil if preferred), by using a small pastry brush (or by tilting over and over again until all the surface is greased). Using a small ladle pour the batter into the skillet. Tip the pan immediately so that the batter covers the entire bottom of the skillet and quickly becomes firm. Cook the crepe for about 1 minute, until it begins to show signs of turning brown around the rim. Turn it over rapidly with a spatula and cook the reverse side for another minute. When the crepe is done, slide it gently onto a flat plate. Brush the skillet once more with melted butter (or oil) and repeat the process until all the crepes are made (about 12).

4. Butter well a large baking dish. Fill each crepe with about 4 to 5 tablespoons of the ratatouille. Roll it up, and place it carefully in the baking dish, one next to the other. When all the crepes are placed in the baking dish, pour the heavy cream over the top, cover the dish with foil, and place it in the oven for about 20 minutes. Serve them hot, allowing 2 crepes per person.

# Crepes with Mushrooms
## (Crêpes aux Champignons)

*Filling*

4 tablespoons butter
1 pound mushrooms, trimmed and
   sliced

1 onion, coarsely chopped
1/3 cup finely chopped fresh parsley
1 cup Béchamel Sauce (page 156)

*Batter*

4 eggs
2 tablespoons olive oil
1¼ cups flour
A pinch of salt

3 cups milk
1–2 teaspoons cold water, if needed
Melted butter (or oil), as needed
½ cup heavy cream

4-6 SERVINGS

1. Heat the butter in a large nonstick skillet over low-medium heat. Add the mushrooms and the onion. Sauté them for about 4–5 minutes, until they begin to turn golden. Stir well and set it aside.

2. Add the parsley to the béchamel sauce and mix well. Add the sauce to the mushrooms and blend the ingredients thoroughly.

3. In a large, deep bowl, mix the eggs, oil, flour, and salt and beat with a mixer, adding 1 cup of milk at a time. The batter must reach the consistency of heavy cream and should be free of flour lumps. If the batter is too thick, add 1–2 teaspoons cold water and continue to mix until it is light and smooth. Refrigerate the batter for an hour or two before starting to use.

4. Preheat the oven to 300°. Heat a 6- or 8-inch crepe skillet over high heat and lightly grease the entire skillet with a bit of melted butter (or oil if preferred), by using a small pastry brush (or by tilting over

and over again until all the surface is greased). Using a small ladle pour the batter into the skillet. Tip the pan immediately so that the batter covers the entire bottom of the skillet and quickly becomes firm. Cook the crepe for about 1 minute, until it begins to show signs of turning brown around the rim. Turn it over rapidly with a spatula and cook the reverse side for another minute. When the crepe is done, slide it gently onto a flat plate. Brush the skillet once more with melted butter (or oil) and repeat the process until all the crepes are made (about 12).

5. Butter thoroughly a long baking dish. Fill each crepe with some of the mushroom-sauce mixture, roll it up, and place it carefully in the baking dish, one next to the other. When all the crepes are in the dish, pour the heavy cream over the top, and place the dish, uncovered, in the oven for about 20 minutes. Serve them hot, allowing 2 crepes per person.

# Crepes with Tomatoes, Herbs, and Goat Cheese Filling

*Crepes*

4 eggs
2 tablespoons vegetable oil
1¼ cups all-purpose flour
A pinch of salt

3 cups milk
½ cup water
Butter (or oil), as needed

*Filling*

½ cup extra-virgin olive oil
8 medium-size tomatoes, coarsely
    chopped
2 onions, chopped
2 garlic cloves, minced
½ cup pitted black olives, chopped

12 ounces goat cheese, crumbled
A bunch of basil leaves, chopped
A bunch of fresh rosemary and
    thyme leaves
Salt and freshly ground black
    pepper to taste

6 SERVINGS

1. Prepare the crepe batter and make the crepes as per the instructions on page 46.

2. Preheat the oven to 300°. To prepare the filling, heat half the oil in a large nonstick skillet over low-medium heat, and add the tomatoes and onions. Sauté lightly for a few minutes, but don't overcook, for tomatoes must remain a bit firm. Stir frequently. At the last minute, add the garlic and olives, stir well again, and turn off the heat. Cover the skillet.

3. Place the goat cheese in a deep bowl, add the remaining ¼ cup olive oil, herbs, salt, and pepper. Mash and mix the ingredients well with a fork. Add the tomato mixture and blend well. Check the seasonings before filling the crepes.

JOY IS THE ECHO OF GOD'S LIFE

WITHIN US.

ABBOT MARMION

4. Generously butter a long baking dish. Fill each crepe with the tomato-cheese mixture, roll it up, and place it carefully in the dish, closely, one next to each other. When all the crepes are arranged on the dish, cover them with aluminum foil and place the dish in the oven for about 15–20 minutes. Serve the crepes hot, allowing 2 crepes per person.

# St. Joseph's Potato Pancakes

5 large red potatoes, peeled and
   grated
2 eggs
²/₃ cup milk
1 onion, grated or finely chopped
Salt and freshly ground black
   pepper to taste

¹/₂ teaspoon dried thyme
A small bunch of parsley, finely
   chopped
About 8 tablespoons vegetable oil
   (or olive oil)
Finely chopped fresh dill, as
   garnish

ABOUT 8 PANCAKES

1.  Preheat the oven to 250°. Place the grated potatoes in a pot, fill it with cold water, and set aside. Drain the potatoes just before using them.

2.  In a deep bowl beat the eggs, add the milk, and beat some more. Add the drained, grated potatoes, onion, salt, and pepper, thyme, and chopped parsley. Mix the ingredients with the help of a spatula until thoroughly blended.

3.  To make the pancakes use a crepe pan or a nonstick skillet. In the pan heat about 1 tablespoon oil (each time) to low-medium and pour in about one eighth of the potato mixture. Flatten the mixture evenly with a spatula and cook over medium heat until the pancake turns brown at the bottom. Turn the pancake over carefully and continue cooking the other side. When the pancake is done, slide it carefully onto an ovenproof platter. Repeat the process until all the pancakes are done. Keep the pancakes in the warm oven until ready to serve. Before serving sprinkle some chopped dill on the top of each pancake.

# Cabbage and Potato Pancakes

½ head small green cabbage
4 large potatoes, peeled and grated
1 medium-size onion, finely
 chopped
2 eggs
¾ cup milk

Salt and freshly ground black
 pepper to taste
A small bunch of parsley, finely
 chopped
About 8 tablespoons vegetable oil
 (or olive oil)

ABOUT 8 PANCAKES

1. Quarter the cabbage and steam it for about 6–7 minutes. Drain and chop the cabbage finely.
2. Place the chopped cabbage, grated potatoes, and chopped onion in a big bowl. Mash them thoroughly with a masher and mix them well with a spatula.
3. In a separate deep bowl beat the eggs. Add the milk and beat some more. Add the cabbage-potato-onion mixture. Add some salt and pepper and the chopped parsley. Mix all the ingredients together until thoroughly blended. Refrigerate for 1 hour.
4. Preheat the oven to 250°. To make the pancakes use a crepe pan or a nonstick skillet. In the pan heat about 1 tablespoon of oil (each time) to low-medium and pour in about one eighth of the potato mixture. Flatten the mixture evenly with a spatula and cook over medium heat until the pancake turns brown at the bottom. Turn the pancake over carefully and continue cooking the other side. When the pancake is done, slide it carefully onto an ovenproof platter. Repeat the process until all the pancakes are done. Keep the pancakes in the warm oven until ready to serve.

# Sweet Potato Pancakes with Eggs

4 large sweet potatoes
2 scallions, finely chopped
A bunch of parsley, finely chopped
3 eggs
1/3 cup milk

Salt and freshly ground black
   pepper to taste
Butter and oil, as needed
4 eggs, as garnish

4 SERVINGS

1. Boil the potatoes for about 15 minutes, or bake them in a preheated oven set at 350° for 25–30 minutes. When they are done, run cold water over them, and allow them to cool for several hours.

2. Peel and mash the potatoes, or grate them in a food processor. Place them in a deep bowl, then add the scallions and the parsley. Mix well.

3. In a separate bowl beat the eggs. Add the milk, salt, and pepper, and blend well. Pour this mixture into the bowl with the potatoes and mix the ingredients well. Refrigerate for at least 2 hours before using.

4. Preheat the oven to 250°. To make the pancakes heat butter and oil in a large nonstick skillet. When the skillet is very hot, lower the heat to low-medium. Pour one quarter of the potato mixture into the skillet, and with a spatula press the mixture down evenly. Try to keep the pancake in a round form. Cook for about 4–5 minutes on each side. (Flip carefully by sliding it onto a plate, then slide it back into the skillet on the other side.) Repeat the entire process three more times. Keep the pancakes in the warm oven until ready to eat.

5. Fry the eggs sunny side up in butter. Sprinkle a dash of salt and pepper over them. Distribute the pancakes on four individual plates, place an egg on the top of each, and serve. It is an ideal dish for a Sunday brunch or a light supper.

## 5

CASSEROLES

# Dutchess County Broccoli and Cheese Casserole

4 medium-size heads broccoli
3 eggs, beaten
1 cup ricotta cheese
1/3 cup grated Cheddar cheese
1 tablespoon cornstarch diluted in
    1/2 cup milk

1 medium-size onion, chopped
Salt and freshly ground black
    pepper to taste

6 SERVINGS

1. Preheat the oven to 350°. Boil the broccoli heads in water to cover for about 10 minutes. Drain them, and then chop them coarsely, including the stems.
2. Beat the eggs in a deep bowl, add the ricotta and Cheddar cheeses, and the cornstarch-milk mixture. Mix thoroughly. Add the chopped onion, salt, and pepper. Add the drained broccoli, mix again, and blend the ingredients well.
3. Butter thoroughly an ovenproof baking dish and place the broccoli mixture in it. Bake for about 30 minutes. Serve hot.

# St. Bede's Broccoli and Potato Casserole

4 medium-size heads broccoli
4 medium-size potatoes, peeled and
    cubed
1 cup milk
3 tablespoons cornstarch (or flour)
3 eggs, beaten

1/2 cup grated mozzarella cheese
Salt and freshly ground black
    pepper to taste
A pinch of nutmeg
Bread crumbs, as needed

6-8 SERVINGS

1. Preheat the oven to 350°. Boil the broccoli heads in water to cover for 8–10 minutes. Drain them, and then chop them coarsely, including the stems. Set them aside.

2. Boil the cubed potatoes in water to cover for about 5 minutes. Drain them and set them aside.

3. Mix thoroughly in a blender (or in a deep bowl) the milk and corn-starch. Add the beaten eggs, cheese, salt, pepper, and nutmeg. Mix or blend the ingredients well.

4. If you have been using a blender, transfer the ingredients to a large bowl. Add the broccoli and potatoes to the egg mixture and with a spatula gently mix the ingredients.

5. Butter well an elongated ovenproof dish. Pour the ingredients in the bowl into the dish and distribute them evenly. Cover the top lightly with bread crumbs. Bake for 30 minutes. Cut it in 6 or 8 even squares and serve it hot.

# St. John Climacus Casserole

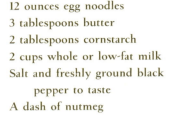

12 ounces egg noodles
3 tablespoons butter
2 tablespoons cornstarch
2 cups whole or low-fat milk
Salt and freshly ground black
    pepper to taste
A dash of nutmeg

1/2 cup crumbled Cheddar cheese
2 cups cut-up cooked asparagus (cut
    into 2-inch pieces)
One 14-ounce jar small onions,
    drained (or frozen, drained)
1/2 cup bread crumbs

4-6 SERVINGS

1. Preheat the oven to 350°. Cook the egg noodles in boiling salted water according to the directions on the package. Drain them.
2. While boiling the noodles, melt the butter in a saucepan. Dilute the cornstarch in the milk and gradually add it to to the pan. Add the salt, pepper, and nutmeg, and continue stirring until the sauce thickens. Add the cheese, and stir until all the cheese is melted.
3. Mix together the asparagus and the small onions in a bowl.
4. Butter thoroughly a shallow baking dish, and alternate layers of the noodles, asparagus-onion mixture, and sauce. (At least two layers of each.)
5. After spreading the sauce evenly over the last asparagus-onion layer, cover the entire top surface with bread crumbs. Bake the casserole for 25–30 minutes maximum. Serve hot.

# Polenta with Broccoli

6 cups water

Salt to taste

2 small heads broccoli, coarsely
    chopped in small pieces

1 onion, finely chopped

2 garlic cloves, minced

4 tablespoons olive oil

1½ cups coarse-ground cornmeal

Freshly ground black pepper to
    taste

3 tablespoons butter

⅓ cup grated Parmesan cheese, plus
    more for sprinkling

6 SERVINGS

1. Pour 3 cups of the water into a good-size saucepan and add the salt and the broccoli. Bring it to a boil. Reduce the heat to low-medium. Cover the saucepan and simmer gently for 15 minutes.

2. Place the onion and garlic in a skillet. Add the oil, and sauté gently for about 2 minutes over low-medium heat. Turn off the heat and set aside.

3. Pour the remaining 3 cups water in another good-size nonstick pan. Add a pinch of salt and bring it to a boil. Drain the broccoli and add its water to the boiling water in the saucepan. Sprinkle the cornmeal gradually into the boiling water, stirring constantly. Continue the process until all the cornmeal is added. Keep stirring until a thick, even consistency is achieved. Turn off the heat.

4. Add to the polenta, the drained broccoli, onion-garlic mixture, pepper, butter, and ⅓ cup of grated Parmesan cheese. Mix the ingredients well. Allow it to cool for at least an hour.

5. Preheat the oven to 300°. Butter thoroughly an elongated ovenproof dish. With a spatula, spread the polenta evenly on the dish. Sprinkle some grated cheese on the top and place it in the oven. Bake for about 20–25 minutes. Allow to cool a bit before serving. During the summer months, this polenta dish can be refrigerated and served cold.

# Jubilate Lentil Loaf

2 cups French green lentils
4 tablespoons olive oil
1 large onion, coarsely chopped
1 cup finely chopped celery
1 large sweet red pepper, finely
  chopped
2 garlic cloves, minced
2 teaspoons dried rosemary

1/2 cup finely chopped fresh parsley
1/2 cup plain tomato sauce
1 cup dried bread crumbs
1/2 cup grated Cheddar cheese
3 extra-large eggs
Salt and freshly ground black
  pepper to taste

6-8 SERVINGS

1. In a good-size saucepan boil the lentils in water to cover until they are cooked, approximately 20 minutes. Drain them thoroughly and set them aside.

2. While the lentils are boiling, pour the olive oil into a large nonstick skillet. Add the onion, celery, and red pepper. Sauté over low-medium heat for about 4–5 minutes, until the vegetables wilt. Turn off the heat. Add the garlic, rosemary, parsley, and tomato sauce. Mix and blend the ingredients well.

3. Preheat the oven to 375°. In a deep bowl mix the bread crumbs and grated cheese together. Set the mixture aside.

4. In a large mixing bowl beat the eggs. Add some salt and pepper and mix well. Add the lentils and mix again. Add the onion mixture and mix once more. Add the bread crumbs and cheese, and mix thoroughly until the ingredients are well blended. Shape the mixture into a loaf.

5. Butter thoroughly a bread pan, and slide the loaf into it. (Reshape the loaf into the pan, if need be.) Place an elongated baking pan in the oven, add several cups of water (do not fill it), and place the lentil loaf in the center. Cook for about 45–50 minutes. The loaf is done when the top turns brown and forms a crust. To be doubly sure, in-

sert a thin knife into the loaf. If the knife comes out clean, the loaf is done.

6. Remove the loaf from the oven, allow it to cool for a few minutes, then unmold by carefully turning it upside down on a platter. Slice and serve.

# Eggplant and Potato Casserole

2 medium-size eggplants, thinly
   sliced
Salt, as needed
8 potatoes, peeled and diced
1/2 cup olive oil
2 large onions, coarsely chopped
4 garlic cloves, chopped
1 red pepper, seeded and thinly
   sliced

2 green bell peppers, seeded and
   diced
1/2 cup finely chopped fresh parsley
Freshly ground black pepper, as
   needed
2 teaspoons paprika
8-10 tomatoes, sliced
Vinegar, as needed
Olive oil, as needed

6-8 SERVINGS

1. Spread a paper towel over a surface, and place the eggplants on the
   top. Sprinkle some salt over them and leave them alone for 30 minutes.

2. In the meantime, place the diced potato in a large saucepan, add water
   to cover and a dash of salt. Bring to a boil, cover the saucepan, and
   simmer for 10 minutes. Drain. It is important that the slices remain
   firm, so do not overcook them.

3. Preheat the oven to 350°. Pour the oil into a large nonstick skillet, add
   the onions, and sauté them about 2–3 minutes over low-medium heat.
   Add the garlic, peppers, and parsley, and continue sautéing and stirring 4–5 minutes longer, until the vegetables soften. Sprinkle on
   some salt and pepper and the paprika, and mix well.

4. Grease thoroughly an ovenproof casserole with butter or oil. Make
   three layers of vegetables, starting at the bottom with the potatoes,
   followed by the eggplants on the top, followed by the onion-pepper
   mixture, followed by the tomato slices. Sprinkle a few drops of
   oil and vinegar on the top. Repeat the layers following the same
   process.

5.  When all the layers are well established, cover the top of the casserole with aluminum foil and bake for about 50–60 minutes. Remove the foil the last 10 minutes of baking and allow the top to brown. Serve the dish hot during the cold weather months, or refrigerate and serve cold during the summer.

# Polenta Savoyarde (POLENTE SAVOYARDE)

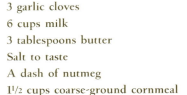

3 garlic cloves
6 cups milk
3 tablespoons butter
Salt to taste
A dash of nutmeg
1½ cups coarse-ground cornmeal

3 eggs
2 ounces grated Parmesan cheese,
    plus more for sprinkling
2 ounces grated Gruyère cheese
Freshly ground black pepper to
    taste

6 SERVINGS

1. Peel the garlic cloves, crush them a bit with a knife, but leave them whole. In a large pot or saucepan, preferably a nonstick one, bring the milk to a boil, then lower the heat to low-medium. Add the garlic, butter, salt, and nutmeg and stir well.

2. When the butter has melted add the cornmeal gradually while stirring continually to prevent the creation of lumps. Continue turning, either with a whisk or spatula, until all the cornmeal is added and the polenta begins to thicken. Lower the heat to low. Continue cooking for several extra minutes, while continuing to stir (about 5–6 minutes). At this point check the consistency of the polenta, to see if needs a bit of extra milk or cornmeal. (Polenta sometimes can be a bit temperamental.)

3. In a deep bowl beat the eggs thoroughly with a mixer, and add them gradually to the polenta while stirring continually. Stir for several minutes.

4. Remove the polenta from the heat. Remove also the garlic cloves. Add the Parmesan and Gruyère cheeses. Add the pepper and with the help of a spatula mix the ingredients thoroughly. Allow the polenta to cool for at least 1 hour.

5. Preheat the oven to 300°. Butter thoroughly an elongated ovenproof dish and spread the polenta over the dish evenly. Run the spatula over the top several times. Sprinkle some Parmesan cheese over the top.

Bake the dish for 15–20 minutes. Serve hot. (During the summer months it can be refrigerated and served cold.)

NOTE: Polenta, being a traditional dish of northern Italy, was naturally adopted in Savoy during the centuries that it was governed by the dukes of Savoy, who were attached to what eventually became Italy.

# Swiss Chard and Mushroom Lasagna

1½ pounds Swiss chard, coarsely
    chopped (including stems)
5 tablespoons olive oil
1 large white onion, coarsely chopped
2½ cups sliced mushrooms
1 garlic clove, minced
1 egg
1 quart low-fat ricotta cheese

2 teaspoons chopped fresh thyme
1 cup fresh basil leaves, chopped
Salt and freshly ground black
    pepper to taste
12 lasagna noodles
5 cups homemade tomato sauce
    (or commercial). See Monastery
    Tomato Sauce (page 166).

4-6 SERVINGS

1. Boil the chard in salted water to cover for about 15–20 minutes, until tender. Drain it. Pour 3 tablespoons of the olive oil into a large skillet and sauté the onion over medium heat for about 2–3 minutes, until it turns golden. Mix the chard and the onion together and set the mixture aside.

2. Preheat the oven to 350°. Pour the remaining 2 tablespoons oil into a nonstick saucepan. Add the mushrooms and garlic. Sauté briefly over low-medium heat for about 2–3 minutes. Stir frequently.

3. Beat egg in a deep bowl, add ricotta, thyme, basil, salt, and pepper, and mix well. Add mushrooms and combine ingredients well.

4. Boil the lasagana noodles in sufficient salted water for about 4–5 minutes maximum. (They must be al dente.) Drain them.

5. Pour 1½ cups tomato sauce in the bottom of a 9 × 9-inch baking dish. Place 4 lasagana noodles over the sauce. Top with a thin layer of the Swiss chard mixture and finish with a thin layer the ricotta-mushroom mixture. Top with 4 more noodles and 1 cup tomato sauce, and repeat the procedure, ending with a layer of noodles and sauce (all of it) on the top. Cover with foil and bake for about 40 minutes. Remove the foil, and continue baking for another 10–15 minutes. Remove from the oven and serve hot.

# Deviled Egg Casserole

One 16-ounce package egg noodles
½ pound spinach (fresh or frozen)
4 ounces (1 stick) butter
    (or margarine)
2 cups milk
½ cup grated mozzarella cheese
6 hard-boiled eggs
2 garlic cloves, peeled and minced

3 tablespoons finely chopped fresh
    parsley
2 tablespoons french mustard
2 tablespoons Worcestershire sauce
3 tablespoons milk (or cream)
Salt and freshly ground black
    pepper to taste
Grated Parmesan cheese, as needed

6 SERVINGS

1. In a casserole cook the noodles in salted boiling water according to the instructions on the package. In another casserole cook the spinach the same way. When cooked, drain the noodles and the spinach. Mix the noodles and the spinach well and place them in a well-buttered elongated baking dish. Spread evenly.

2. Preheat the oven to 375°. Melt the butter in another casserole and gradually stir in the milk and the mozzarella cheese. Stir continually over low-medium heat until a creamy sauce is formed.

3. Slice the eggs in half lengthwise and remove the yolks. Place the yolks in a deep bowl. Add the garlic, parsley, mustard, Worcestershire sauce, milk, salt, and pepper. Mash and mix the ingredients well.

4. Fill the egg whites with the yolk mixture. Distribute the eggs evenly on the top of the noodle-spinach mixture. Pour the cheese sauce over it, making sure the top surface is covered evenly. Sprinkle some Parmesan cheese over the whole top.

5. Place the dish in the oven for about 30–40 minutes, until the top turns golden brown. Remove the casserole from the oven, allow it to rest and cool a bit for about 2 or 3 minutes. Serve immediately after.

# Eggplant Tian (Tian d'Aubergines)

4 medium-size eggplants, trimmed
Salt, as needed
4 eggs
Bread crumbs, as needed
Vegetable oil, as needed
2 cups tomato sauce. See Monastery Tomato Sauce (page 166).

A pinch of dried thyme
A pinch of chopped basil
4 garlic cloves, minced
Freshly ground black pepper to taste
Grated Parmesan cheese

6 SERVINGS

1. Cut the eggplants in thin slices lengthwise. Place them in a long flat dish. Sprinkle salt over them, and set them aside for at least 1 hour.
2. Preheat the oven to 350°. Beat the eggs in a deep bowl and spread the bread crumbs in a flat plate. Dip each eggplant slice in the beaten eggs, then dip both sides in the bread crumbs. Pour the oil into a large nonstick skillet. Heat it to medium-high. When the oil is really hot, fry both sides of the slices well. As they are done, place them on a dish covered with paper towels.
3. While the eggplants are frying, pour the tomato sauce into a saucepan, add the herbs, garlic, and pepper. Cook for about 8–10 minutes, over low-medium heat. Then turn it off.
4. Oil thoroughly an elongated ovenproof casserole dish. Cover the bottom of the dish with a third of the eggplant slices. Cover the eggplants with a third of the tomato sauce. Sprinkle some grated cheese on the top. Repeat the layers twice more.
5. Pour the rest of the beaten eggs over the top layer and spread evenly with a spatula. Place the dish in the oven for about 30 minutes. When the tian is done, allow it to cool for about 2 or 3 minutes before serving.

# Swiss Chard Tian

1 pound Swiss chard, trimmed
Olive oil, as needed
1 onion, coarsely chopped
3 garlic cloves, minced
3 eggs

Salt and freshly ground black
    pepper to taste
4 teaspoons water
Bread crumbs, as needed

4-6 SERVINGS

1. Chop the Swiss chard, both leaves and stems, and then boil the chard for about 20 minutes in lightly salted water. Drain the chard and set it aside.
2. Preheat the oven to 350°. Pour some olive oil into a large skillet. Add the onion and sauté lightly over low-medium heat for 2–3 minutes. Add the garlic, and sauté for another minute. Add the Swiss chard and continue sautéing for 2–3 minutes more, blending the ingredients well.
3. Beat the eggs in a deep bowl, add the salt, pepper, and water. Mix well.
4. Butter thoroughly a long ovenproof dish. Place the chard mixture in it and spread evenly. Pour the egg mixture on the top and also spread evenly. Sprinkle some bread crumbs over the top surface. Place the dish in the oven for about 25–30 minutes. Serve hot.

# Zucchini Tian

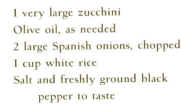

1 very large zucchini
Olive oil, as needed
2 large Spanish onions, chopped
1 cup white rice
Salt and freshly ground black
     pepper to taste

1 teaspoon dried thyme
2 cups water
4 eggs
1/2 cup milk
Bread crumbs, as needed

6 SERVINGS

1. Preheat the oven to 350°. Cut the zucchini in 3/4-inch-thick slices. Pour some oil into a large frying pan set over medium-high heat, and fry both sides of the zucchini slices. The slices must remain firm, so do not overdo the frying part. As they get done, place them on a dish covered with a paper towel. Set aside.

2. Next, add oil to the pan, and sauté the onions over low-medium heat for about 3–4 minutes until they begin to wilt. Set aside.

3. While the zucchini is being fried, place the rice in a saucepan, add 2 teaspoons oil, and mix well. Add some salt and pepper and the dried thyme. Add the water, stir a few times, and then cook the rice, covered, over low-medium heat. When the rice is done, turn off the heat.

4. Beat the eggs thoroughly, add the milk and a dash of salt and pepper, and blend the ingredients well.

5. Butter or oil thoroughly an elongated ovenproof dish deep enough to hold the vegetable and rice layers. Cover the bottom of the dish with half the zucchini slices, then spread over them half the sautéed onions and spread half the rice over the onions. Repeat the layers once more with the remaining zucchini, onions, and rice.

6. Pour the egg mixture evenly over the layers and allow it to reach the bottom of the dish. Let stand for 10 minutes, then spread some bread crumbs over the top. Place the dish in the oven for about 30 minutes. When the tian is done, allow it to cool for about 3 minutes before serving.

RICE, PASTA, COUSCOUS

# Mushroom and Wild Rice Pilaf

6 tablespoons olive oil
1 onion, finely chopped
8 mushrooms, thinly sliced
2 garlic cloves, finely minced
Rind of 1 lemon, finely minced
1½ cups wild rice

3 cups vegetable stock (or water)
Salt and freshly ground black
    pepper to taste
Finely chopped fresh chervil, as
    garnish

4-6 SERVINGS

1. Pour the olive oil into a nonstick pot, add the onion and mushrooms, and sauté them lightly over low-medium heat until they soften. Add the garlic and lemon rind, and stir all the ingredients well for about 1 minute.

2. At this point, add the rice, stock or water, salt, and pepper, and over medium heat bring to a quick boil. Reduce the heat to low-medium, stir the ingredients, cover the pot, and simmer slowly until all the liquid is absorbed (about 30–40 minutes).

3. When the rice is done, check the seasonings and serve immediately. Garnish the top with some chopped chervil.

# Chickpeas and Spinach Risotto

5 tablespoons olive oil
1 onion, finely chopped
2 garlic cloves, minced
4 mushrooms, finely chopped
4 cups vegetable stock (or water)
1 cup dry white wine
1 cup Arborio rice

½ cup drained canned chickpeas
2 cups finely chopped spinach
Salt and freshly ground black
   pepper to taste
⅓ cup grated Parmesan cheese
   (or Romano)

4 SERVINGS

1. In a large nonstick saucepan, heat the oil over low-medium heat, and sauté the onion. When the onion begins to turn golden, add the garlic and mushrooms. Mix well.

2. While sautéing the onion, bring the vegetable stock or water to a boil. Add the wine. After the stock boils, lower the heat to low and simmer gently. (Keep simmering throughout.)

3. Add the rice to the onion mixture, and make sure the rice is well coated. Stir continually. Add 1 cup of the stock-wine mixture and raise the heat to medium. Continue to stir until almost all the liquid part is absorbed.

4. Add the chickpeas and 1 more cup of the stock-wine mixture. Continue stirring for another 4 or 5 minutes, adding more stock-wine mixture as needed. The rice must be kept moist at all times.

5. Add the spinach and continue adding the remainder of the stock-wine mixture gradually, all the while continuing to stir. Before adding the last cup of stock, add some salt and pepper. Continue stirring until all the liquid is absorbed. Check the seasonings.

6. Remove the saucepan from the heat, add the cheese, and stir gently a few times. Cover the saucepan and set aside for about 5 minutes before serving. Serve hot.

# Rice, Herb, and Cheese Croquettes

2 cups Arborio rice
4 cups water
A dash of salt
1 tablespoon butter
4 eggs
Freshly ground black pepper to taste
1 teaspoon fresh thyme (or 1/2 teaspoon dried)
2 teaspoons chopped fresh chives (or 1 teaspoon dried)

4 tablespoons finely chopped fresh parsley (or 2 tablespoons dried)
1 teaspoon dried oregano
1 1/4 cups dried bread crumbs
1/2 cup grated Gruyère cheese (or other cheese of your choice—Parmesan, Romano, etc.)
Vegetable oil (or olive oil), as needed, for deep frying

6-8 SERVINGS

1. Preheat the oven to 150°. Place the rice in a good-size saucepan. Add the water and salt and bring to a boil. Cook over low-medium heat until all the liquid is absorbed. When the rice is done add 1 tablespoon butter and mix well. Place the rice in a dish and allow it to cool.

2. Break the eggs into a deep bowl. Add salt and pepper and beat with a whisk or a mixer. Add all the herbs and mix well with a fork.

3. Add the rice, 3/4 cup of the bread crumbs, and the cheese to the egg mixture and mix the ingredients well. Set it aside for 1 hour.

4. Then, moisten your hands with water and shape the rice mixture into approximately 2-inch croquettes by rolling carefully with both hands. Coat the croquettes with the remaining 1/2 cup bread crumbs.

5. Pour some oil into a deep, nonstick skillet and heat it on high for a deep-fry. Fry the croquettes in small batches, taking care so that they are equally cooked and brown on all sides. When the croquettes are done place them one by one on the top of a paper towel to dry. Transfer the croquettes to an ovenproof dish and place them in the warm oven until ready to serve. Serve hot.

# Rice Tortillitas (TORTILLITAS DE ARROZ)

4 eggs
1 1/2 cups milk
3/4 cup cooked rice
1/3 cup grated Parmigiano-Reggiano
    cheese
2 shallots, finely minced

A few sprigs of parsley, finely
    chopped
Salt and freshly ground black
    pepper to taste
Olive oil (or vegetable oil) for deep
    frying, as needed

SEVERAL YIELDINGS

1. Preheat the oven to 200°. In a deep bowl mix the eggs with a whisk or mixer. Add the milk and mix some more.
2. Add the cooked rice, cheese, shallots, parsley, salt, and pepper. Mix and blend the ingredients well with a fork. Refrigerate for 1 hour.
3. Pour some oil into a large skillet and heat it over medium-high heat. When the oil is hot, spoon the rice mixture into it—each one exactly the size of a large full round spoon (circular)—and deep fry it. Leave space in between them. When one side is done, turn it over with a spatula and cook the other side. As they are cooked, remove them from the skillet and place them in a dish. Keep them warm in the oven until ready to serve. They make wonderful appetizers.

# Mediterranean Vegetarian Paella

8 tablespoons olive oil, more if needed
1 onion, finely chopped
1 tomato, peeled, seeded, and chopped
3 garlic cloves, minced
2 red peppers, roasted, peeled, and chopped
1/2 cup shelled peas
12 pitted green olives, chopped
1/3 cup capers
12 mushrooms, trimmed and sliced in halves
2 cups Arborio rice
1 teaspoon paprika
A pinch of saffron
6 cups boiling vegetable broth (or water)
Salt and freshly ground black pepper to taste

6 SERVINGS

1. Heat the oil in a heavy cast-iron skillet. Add the onion, tomato, and garlic, and sauté briefly over low heat for 1–2 minutes. Stir frequently.
2. Add the peppers, peas, olives, capers, and mushrooms. Continue sautéing for another 2 minutes. Add the rice, paprika, and saffron and stir continually for 1–2 minutes until the rice is fully coated and begins to change color.
3. Pour in the boiling broth or water and raise the heat to medium. Add some salt and pepper. Stir frequently. Cook for about 15 minutes, then lower the heat to low-medium until the rice is cooked. Once the rice is cooked, cover the saucepan, turn off the heat, and let it rest for 3–4 minutes before serving. (You may add a bit more water if necessary, or even 1/2 cup of dry white wine on festive occasions.)

# Pasta with Arugula and Goat Cheese Sauce

A bunch of fresh arugula
4 sprigs of fresh parsley
One 8-ounce container low-fat
    yogurt or sour cream
1/3 cup goat cheese, crumbled

Salt and freshly ground black
    pepper to taste
16 ounces fusilli noodles
Grated Parmesan cheese, as garnish

4 SERVINGS

1. Before preparing the sauce, fill a large casserole with water, and bring the water to a boil.
2. Wash and clean well the arugula and the parsley. Dry thoroughly. Trim and chop both the arugula and the parsley.
3. Place the arugula and the parsley in a food processor. Add the yogurt or sour cream, goat cheese, salt, and pepper. Blend the ingredients thoroughly. Keep the sauce at room temperature until ready to use. (It should be made about a half hour or so before you use it.)
4. Add a pinch of salt to the boiling water, and cook the fusilli noodles following the instructions on the package. When the noodles are cooked, drain them, and place them in four serving dishes. Pour the sauce evenly over the top of each serving and add some cheese to each dish. Serve immediately.

# Linguine Noodles in Spicy Sauce

1/3 cup olive oil, plus 2 tablespoons
  for the pasta water
1 onion, coarsely chopped
10 plum tomatoes, peeled, seeded,
  and chopped
4 garlic cloves, peeled and minced
1 small dried chile pepper,
  crumbled

1/4 cup fresh basil leaves, finely
  chopped
Salt to taste
1 pound linguine noodles
Grated Parmesan or Romano
  cheese, for serving

6-8 SERVINGS

1. Prepare the sauce by heating the 1/3 cup of olive oil in a good-size pot. Add the onion, tomatoes, garlic, chile pepper, basil, and salt. Cook over medium heat for about 15–20 minutes. Stir often and lower the heat to low-medium for the last 10 minutes.

2. In a large saucepan bring the water for cooking the linguine to a boil and add a dash of salt. Throw the noodles into the water, add the remaining 2 tablespoons olive oil, and cook for about 5–6 minutes. The noodles must remain al dente. Drain them.

3. In a large bowl mix the noodles and the sauce well. Serve hot, and pass around a bowl of grated cheese.

# Lemon-Scented Spaghetti

1 fennel bulb, thinly sliced
1 pound spaghetti noodles
1/3 cup olive oil, plus 1 tablespoon
A dash of salt
20 black olives, pitted
4 garlic cloves, peeled
4 tablespoons lemon juice

1 teaspoon finely grated lemon zest
A few sprigs of parsley, chopped
Salt and freshly ground black
    pepper to taste
About 1/3 cup olive oil
Optional: grated cheese, for serving

4-6 SERVINGS

1. Fill a good-size saucepan with water, bring water to a boil, and add the fennel, spaghetti, 1 tablespoon of the olive oil, and salt. Cook according to the instructions on the spaghetti package.

2. While the spaghetti is cooking prepare the sauce by placing the olives, garlic, lemon juice, lemon zest, and parsley in a small food processor. Blend the ingredients well.

3. Heat the remaining 1/3 cup olive oil in a large, heavy-based, deep pan. Add the olive-lemon mixture and sauté briefly for a minute or two over low-medium heat, while stirring constantly. Add the spaghetti-fennel mixture and some salt and pepper, and mix with care until the noodles are evenly coated with the sauce. Serve hot, and if you like, pass a bowl of grated cheese at the table.

# Farfalle Piamontese

1 pound farfalle (butterfly) noodles
A bunch of fresh arugula, trimmed
1 tablespoon olive oil
A dash of salt
1/3 cup extra-virgin olive oil
2 medium-size zucchini, thinly
   sliced
1 cup red cherry tomatoes, sliced in
   halves
1 cup yellow cherry tomatoes,
   sliced in halves
2 garlic cloves, minced
1 teaspoon dried oregano (or 2
   teaspoons fresh)
Salt and freshly ground black
   pepper to taste
Grated Pecorino Romano cheese,
   for serving

4-6 SERVINGS

1. Add the farfalle pasta to a large saucepan of rapidly boiling water. Add the arugula, 1 tablespoon olive oil, and salt and follow the instructions on the farfalle package for cooking time. The pasta must remain al dente.

2. Pour 1/3 cup extra-virgin olive oil into a large nonstick skillet. Add the zucchini and sauté them for about 4–5 minutes over low-medium heat. Stir frequently. Just before serving, add the cherry tomatoes, garlic, oregano, salt, and pepper, and sauté briefly for only 1 minute. Be careful to see that the tomatoes remain intact.

3. Drain the pasta, and then mix it with the sauce. (Toss carefully because of the tomatoes.) Serve hot and sprinkle grated cheese on the top.

# Tagliatelle with Chickpeas

2 cups dried chickpeas
1 teaspoon baking soda
8 cups water, more if needed
3 tablespoons olive oil
A dash of salt
A branch of rosemary
5 garlic cloves, minced
1 pound tagliatelle noodles

10 tablespoons extra-virgin olive oil,
    more if needed
1 tablespoon balsamic vinegar
A bunch of fresh parsley, finely
    chopped
Freshly ground black pepper to
    taste
Grated Pecorino or Parmesan
    cheese, for serving

4-6 SERVINGS

1. Place the chickpeas in a container filled with water. Add 1 teaspoon baking soda and soak overnight.
2. The following day, drain and rinse the chickpeas. Place them in a large saucepan, add 8 cups water, 3 tablespoons olive oil, salt, and rosemary. Bring the water to a boil and then lower the heat to medium. Cover the saucepan and cook about 3 hours. Add more water if needed.
3. Toward the end of the cooking process, when the chickpeas are tender, add more water to the saucepan as necessary. Bring to a boil, add the garlic and tagliatelle noodles, lower the heat to medium, and cook the pasta according to the instructions on the package. Don't overcook—the pasta must be al dente. When the pasta is cooked, drain everything, and remove the rosemary.
4. Heat the extra-virgin olive oil to low-medium in a saucepan. Add the balsamic vinegar, chickpeas, noodles, chopped parsley, salt, and pepper. Toss gently and see that the peas and noodles are well coated with the oil. Serve hot. Pass a bowl of grated cheese to accompany the pasta at the table.

# Fettuccine de Norcia

1 pound fettuccine noodles
7 tablespoons olive oil
A dash of salt
3 garlic cloves, minced
3 tomatoes, peeled and chopped

1/2 cup pitted black olives, coarsely
    chopped
6 tablespoons capers
1/4 cup dry white wine
16 fresh basil leaves, finely
    chopped

*Optional:*

One 2-ounce can anchovies, drained
    and finely chopped

Salt and freshly ground black
    pepper to taste
Grated Romano cheese, for
    serving

4-6 SERVINGS

1. Fill a large saucepan with water and bring to a boil. Add the fettuccine, 2 tablespoons of the olive oil, and salt. Cook the noodles according to the instructions on the package. Remember that pasta should
   always be al dente. Drain.

2. In the meantime, while the fettuccine is boiling, pour the remaining 5
   tablespoons olive oil into a good-size nonstick skillet and add the garlic. Sauté for 1 minute over low-medium heat. Stir continually. Add
   the tomatoes, olives, and capers. Continue sautéing for another 3 minutes. Stir often.

3. When the tomatoes begin to wilt and turn into a sauce, add the wine,
   basil, anchovies, and some salt and pepper. Stir, cover the skillet, and
   continue cooking for another 5–6 minutes.

4. Return the drained fettuccine to the saucepan. Pour the sauce over it
   and toss gently, making sure all the noodles get coated and the sauce is

evenly distributed. Serve hot and pass a bowl of grated Romano cheese at the table for those who wish to add it to the pasta.

NOTE: Norcia is the birthplace of St. Benedict and his twin sister, St. Scholastica. This dish is a specialty of the town, where the locals love to enhance the sauce by adding black truffles to it.

# Linguine di Parma

1 pound linguine noodles
A dash of salt
16 asparagus spears, trimmed
3 tablespoons butter
4 tablespoons finely chopped fresh
parsley

3 tablespoons finely chopped fresh
basil
2/3 cup heavy cream
Freshly ground pepper to taste
1/3 cup grated Parmesan cheese, plus
more for serving

6 SERVINGS

1. Cook the linguine in a good-size saucepan of boiling water. Add salt. Cook according to the instructions on the linguine package. Drain.
2. While the pasta is boiling, slice the asparagus into 2-inch pieces. Heat the butter over medium heat in a large nonstick skillet, add the asparagus pieces, and sauté them for about 3 minutes. Stir frequently.
3. Add the parsley, basil, heavy cream, and some salt and pepper. Stir continually for about 2–3 minutes. Add the grated cheese and mix well.
4. When ready to serve, pour the sauce with the asparagus into the saucepan containing the linguine and toss gently, making sure the pasta is well coated with the sauce. Serve hot, accompanied by a bowl of grated cheese for those who wish to add a bit more to their pasta.

# Gnocchi with Mushrooms and Zucchini

One 14-ounce package frozen
   gnocchi
4 tablespoons olive oil
A dash of salt
16 mushrooms, cleaned and
   trimmed
2 small- to medium-size zucchini
2 shallots (or 1 small vidalia onion)
2 garlic cloves, peeled

4 tablespoons butter
2 tablespoons water
⅓ cup dry white wine
A few sprigs of parsley, finely
   chopped
Freshly ground black pepper to
   taste
Grated Romano cheese, as garnish

4 SERVINGS

1. Bring a large saucepan of water to a boil. Add the gnocchi, 1 table-spoon of the olive oil, and the salt. Cook the gnocchi over medium heat, following the directions on the package, usually about 3 minutes. When cooked, drain the gnocchi and keep them covered.

2. Slice the mushrooms in even halves from top to bottom. Slice the zucchini in four even parts lengthwise, and then cut the long slices in cubes. Chop the shallots and mince the garlic.

3. Melt the butter in a large nonstick skillet, and add the mushrooms and zucchini. Cook over low heat for about 4 minutes, stirring often. Add the shallots, garlic, the remaining 3 tablespoons olive oil, and the water. Mix well and continue cooking for another minute. Add the wine, parsley, salt, and pepper. Mix well and cook for 2 minutes more. Add the gnocchi. Mix again, cover the skillet, and cook for 2–3 minutes longer. Turn the heat off.

4. Place the gnocchi and vegetables on hot plates. Sprinkle some grated cheese on top, and serve immediately.

# Gnocchi with Arugula and Watercress

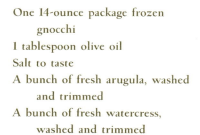

LIFE, HOWEVER SHORT

IS MADE STILL SHORTER

BY WASTE OF TIME.

SAMUEL JOHNSON

One 14-ounce package frozen
    gnocchi
1 tablespoon olive oil
Salt to taste
A bunch of fresh arugula, washed
    and trimmed
A bunch of fresh watercress,
    washed and trimmed

1 garlic clove, crushed
6 tablespoons extra-virgin olive oil,
    more if needed
Freshly ground black pepper to
    taste
Grated Pecorino Romano cheese,
    for serving

4 SERVINGS

1. Bring a large saucepan of water to a boil. Add the gnocchi, 1 table-spoon of oil, and salt. Cook the gnocchi over medium heat, following the directions on the package. Midway through the cooking add half of the arugula and half of the watercress. When cooked, drain and keep the gnocchi and the greens covered.

2. Rub the crushed garlic thoroughly into a large nonstick skillet, and then discard it. Pour the olive oil into the skillet and heat it. Add the remaining arugula and watercress (the stems trimmed) and sauté lightly over low-medium heat for a few minutes, until they wilt. Add the gnocchi mixture and the pepper and toss gently until the ingredients are well mixed. Place the gnocchi on warm plates, top each serving with the grated cheese, and serve immediately. Pass a bowl of grated cheese at the table for those who wish to add more to their pasta.

# Rigatoni with Eggplants

1/3 cup olive oil, plus 2 tablespoons
2 medium-size eggplants, cubed
10 plum tomatoes, peeled and
    chopped
1 onion, chopped
3 garlic cloves, minced

1 bay leaf
Several fresh basil leaves, chopped
Salt and freshly ground black
    pepper to taste
1 pound rigatoni noodles
Grated Romano cheese, as garnish

6-8 SERVINGS

1. Pour 1/3 cup of the olive oil into a good-size nonstick saucepan. Add the vegetables, heat to medium, and cook for a few minutes, while stirring often. Add the bay leaf, basil, and the salt and pepper. Mix well, lower the heat to low-medium, and cover the saucepan. Cook for about 20 minutes, stirring occasionally. Check the seasonings. Remove the bay leaf when the sauce is done.

2. While making the sauce, fill a good-size saucepan with water and bring it to a boil. Add the remaining 2 tablespoons olive oil and some salt. Add the rigatoni and cook the noodles according to the directions on the package. The pasta must be al dente. Drain.

3. Mix the pasta and the sauce well, so that the pasta is thoroughly coated with the sauce. Transfer the pasta-sauce mixture to a heated serving dish. Sprinkle the grated cheese on top and serve hot. You may wish to serve some extra grated cheese at the table. Place it in a bowl and pass it around.

# Fusilli Noodles in Fiery Sauce

7 tablespoons extra-virgin olive oil
4 garlic cloves, peeled and minced
10 plum tomatoes, peeled and
    chopped
1 large onion, chopped
2 red chile peppers, minced
1 teaspoon cumin

12 fresh basil leaves, coarsely
    chopped
A few sprigs of Italian parsley,
    minced
Salt to taste
14 ounces fusilli noodles
Grated Parmesan cheese, for serving

4-6 SERVINGS

1. Heat 6 tablespoons of the olive oil in a large nonstick saucepan. Add the garlic, sauté it alone for 30 seconds, then add the tomatoes, onion, and chile peppers and cook over medium heat for about 12–15 minutes, stirring often, until the tomatoes turn into a sauce.

2. Add the cumin, basil, parsley, and salt and continue cooking and stirring for another 5 minutes or so, over low-medium heat. Check the seasonings and the even consistency of the sauce. It should be smooth and fiery.

3. While the sauce is being made, fill a large saucepan with water and add a dash of salt. When the water reaches the boiling point, add the fusilli noodles and the remaining 1 tablespoon olive oil. Follow the instructions on the package about the boiling time, remembering always that the pasta should be eaten al dente.

4. When the fusilli are cooked, drain them, and then toss them into the saucepan with the sauce. Mix well, and serve immediately, on hot plates, accompanied by a bowl of cheese at the table.

# Couscous with Portobello Mushrooms

4 tablespoons olive oil

4 shallots, trimmed and thinly
   sliced

8 portobello mushrooms, cleaned
   and thinly sliced

2 cups vegetable stock (or water)

1 cup wheat couscous

Salt and white pepper to taste

4-6 SERVINGS

1. Heat the oil in a nonstick casserole, and sauté the shallots over low-medium heat for about 2 minutes. Stir continually.

2. Add the sliced mushrooms and continue to cook for about another 3 minutes until the mushrooms soften.

3. Add the vegetable stock, or water, and bring to a boil. Add the couscous, salt, and pepper, and stir continually for about 2 or 3 minutes. Turn off the heat, cover the casserole, and let the couscous stand for about 5–6 minutes, until the liquid has been absorbed and the couscous is done. Serve it hot.

# Couscous with Corn and Mint

## ( COLD SALAD )

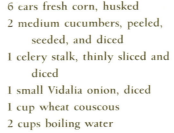

6 ears fresh corn, husked
2 medium cucumbers, peeled, seeded, and diced
1 celery stalk, thinly sliced and diced
1 small Vidalia onion, diced
1 cup wheat couscous
2 cups boiling water

Salt and freshly ground black pepper to taste
A bunch of fresh mint, finely chopped
A bunch of fresh cilantro, finely chopped
8 tablespoons olive oil
4 teaspoons lemon juice

6 SERVINGS

1. Fill a large soup pot with water and place the ears of corn in the pot. Boil for about 5–6 minutes. Remove the corn and set it aside to cool. When the corn has cooled, cut the kernels from the cobs by using a sharp knife to remove the kernels. Place the corn kernels in a big, deep bowl.

2. Add the cucumbers, celery, and onion to the bowl.

3. Cook the couscous in the boiling water, over medium heat, for about 3 minutes. Stir continually. Turn off the heat, cover the pot, and let the couscous stand for several minutes until all the water has been absorbed and the couscous is done.

4. Add the couscous to the vegetables in the bowl. Add the salt and pepper, the finely chopped mint and cilantro, and the olive oil, and the lemon juice. Toss the ingredients well and place the bowl in the refrigerator for several hours before serving. Serve cold. It is an exciting dish for a summer picnic or a meal outdoors.

## 7

VEGETABLES

# Flageolet Beans à la Lyonnaise

DON'T TALK UNLESS YOU CAN

IMPROVE THE SILENCE.

OLD NEW ENGLAND SAYING

1 pound dried flageolet beans,
  soaked overnight
8 cups water
2 carrots, peeled and diced
1 large whole onion, stuck with 4
  cinnamon cloves

1 bay leaf
Salt to taste
2 garlic cloves, finely chopped
1/3 cup finely chopped fresh parsley
2 1/2 tablespoons butter
White pepper to taste

6-8 SERVINGS

1. Drain and rinse the soaked beans. Place the beans in a large casserole. Add the water, carrots, whole onion, bay leaf, and salt. Bring the water to a boil, then lower the heat to low-medium and cook for about 1 hour to 1 hour and 30 minutes. Cover the pot and stir occasionally.

2. After about 1 hour remove the bay leaf and the whole onion with the cloves. Add the garlic, parsley, butter, and white pepper. Cover the pot and continue cooking for another 5 minutes. Drain the remaining liquid and serve the beans hot.

# Stuffed Red Peppers Basque Style

( PIMENTS FARCIS À LA BASQUAISE )

3 good-size red peppers
3 tablespoons olive oil
1 medium-size onion, chopped
2 garlic cloves, minced
2 hard-boiled eggs, crumbled
One 8-ounce can light tuna fish,
    drained and crumbled

6 sprigs of parsley, finely chopped
2 eggs, beaten
Salt and freshly ground black
    pepper to taste
Bread crumbs, as needed

6 SERVINGS

1. Preheat the oven to 350°. Slice the peppers lengthwise in perfect halves and carefully scoop out the insides. Place them in a well-buttered ovenproof dish.

2. Pour the oil into a nonstick frying pan. Add the onion and garlic and sauté them lightly over low-medium heat for no more than 2 minutes.

3. Place the crumbled hard-boiled eggs in a bowl, add the crumbled tuna, chopped parsley, onion-garlic mixture, beaten eggs, salt, and pepper. Mix the ingredients well.

4. Stuff the hollow peppers evenly with the tuna-egg mixture. Cover each top lightly with bread crumbs. Place the dish in the oven and bake for about 25 minutes. Serve hot.

# Stuffed Tomatoes Montpellier

SIMPLICITY AND STILLNESS ARE THE

CORRECT PRINCIPLES FOR MANKIND.

SAYINGS OF LAO-TZU (6TH CENTURY)

6 medium-size ripe tomatoes
18 large lettuce leaves
Montpellier Dip (page 7)

5 tablespoons mayonnaise,
homemade or commercial

6 SERVINGS

1. Clean the tomatoes well. Slice them at the very top and carefully scoop out their insides.
2. To prepare a Montpellier sauce, add 5 tablespoons mayonnaise to the Montpellier Dip and mix the ingredients well.
3. When ready to serve, place 3 lettuce leaves on each plate in the form of a clover leaf, and on the center place a tomato. Fill each of them with the Montpellier sauce. Serve it cold during the summer months as an appetizer, when tomatoes are in season.

# Stuffed Tomatoes Bidart

(TOMATES FARCIES DE BIDART)

8 medium-size ripe tomatoes
7 tablespoons olive oil
5 medium-size onions, chopped
2 medium-size red peppers, diced
Salt and freshly ground black
    pepper to taste

A few sprigs of parsley, finely
    chopped
Bread crumbs, as needed

8 SERVINGS

1. Preheat the oven to 350°. Wash and dry the tomatoes. Evenly slice off the tops of the tomatoes and discard them. Scoop out the tomato insides carefully with the help of a pointed spoon. Place the tomato shells upside down on a plate for about 15 minutes to drain their remaining liquid.

2. Pour the olive oil into a large frying pan or saucepan, add the onions, peppers, about one third of the tomato pulp, salt, pepper, and parsley. Cook over low-medium heat, stirring occasionally until the onions begin to turn golden and a saucy consistency is achieved.

3. Fill each tomato with the onion mixture and place them in a well-oiled ovenproof dish. Sprinkle some bread crumbs over the top of each tomato and place them in the oven for 30 minutes. Serve hot.

# Spanish Lima Beans (HABAS A LA ESPAÑOLA)

2 pounds young lima beans (fresh
   or frozen)
10 tablespoons olive oil
1 large Spanish onion, chopped
1 large red pepper, seeded and
   diced
5 garlic cloves, peeled and minced
A dash of salt

1/2 cup water
Freshly ground black pepper to
   taste
3 hard-boiled eggs, coarsely
   chopped
A few sprigs of parsley, finely
   chopped, as garnish

4-6 SERVINGS

1.  Shell the lima beans and set them aside.
2.  Pour the oil into a large nonstick casserole. Add the onion and pepper. Sauté briefly for about 2–3 minutes, over low-medium heat, until the onions turn lightly golden.
3.  Add the garlic, beans, salt, and 1/2 cup water. Stir gently, cover the casserole, and continue cooking for about 15 minutes, until most of the water is absorbed and the beans are cooked. Drain whatever liquid remains.
4.  Place the bean mixture in a serving bowl. Add the pepper, chopped eggs, and fresh parsley. Toss gently and serve.

OPTION: Meat eaters may add 1 cup cubed smoked ham if they wish. Usually the dish is prepared with ham or bacon. The above recipe is my vegetarian version of it.

BE NOT ANGRY THAT YOU CANNOT MAKE OTHERS AS YOU WISH THEM TO BE, SINCE YOU CANNOT MAKE YOURSELF AS YOU WISH TO BE.

THOMAS À KEMPIS

# Baked Tomatoes with Eggs

6 large ripe tomatoes
Salt and freshly ground black
   pepper to taste
A pinch of thyme (fresh or dried)
6 teaspoons finely chopped fresh
   parsley

6 large eggs
6 teaspoons extra-virgin olive oil
   plus more for the baking dish
Grated cheese, as needed (Romano,
   Gruyère, etc.)

6 SERVINGS

1. Preheat the oven to 300°. Wash and dry the tomatoes. Evenly slice off the tops and set them aside. Carefully scoop out the tomato insides, and then place them upside down on a paper towel for about 15 minutes to drain.

2. Sprinkle a bit of salt, pepper, thyme, and 1 teaspoon of the parsley inside each tomato. Carefully break an egg into each one. Pour 1 teaspoon olive oil over each egg. Sprinkle a pinch of salt and pepper, and some grated cheese over the eggs and cover them with the reserved tomato tops.

3. Pour some olive oil into a baking dish and spread it thoroughly with a small brush. Place the tomatoes in the dish, and bake for about 25–30 minutes. Serve hot. (Remove the tops before serving.)

# Red Kidney Beans in Wine Sauce

1 pound dried red kidney beans
2 large white onions, chopped
1 sprig of fresh thyme
3 sprigs of fresh parsley
1 bay leaf
1 teaspoon salt
3 tablespoons sweet butter

2 cups red wine
1/3 cup olive oil
1 cup tomato sauce
6 garlic cloves, peeled and minced
Freshly ground black pepper to
    taste

6 SERVINGS

1. Soak the beans overnight, then rinse and drain them under cold running water.

2. Place the beans and one chopped white onion in a large casserole, add plenty of water, tie up the thyme, parsley, and bay leaf into a bouquet garni, and add it to the beans. Add 1 teaspoon salt and bring the water to a quick boil. Reduce the heat to medium and cook the beans, partially covered, for about $1^{1}/2$ hours until the beans are tender. Stir from time to time and when they are done drain them of any remaining juice. Also remove the bouquet garni.

3. During the last 30 minutes of the beans' cooking time, melt the butter in a good-size, nonstick casserole and sauté the other chopped onion for about 2–3 minutes over low-medium heat. Add the wine, olive oil, tomato sauce, and garlic. Mix well and simmer gently while the beans continue to cook in the other casserole.

4. Add the drained beans to the wine-tomato mixture, season them with salt and pepper, mix well, and continue cooking the beans until they absorb all the liquid. Cook them uncovered and stir occasionally, making sure the beans don't stick to the bottom. When the beans are done, check the seasonings again and serve them hot.

# Zucchini Beignets

4 medium-size zucchini
2 cups white flour
4 tablespoons cornstarch
1 tablespoon baking powder

Salt and white pepper to taste
2 cups cold dark beer
Olive oil, as needed, for deep
 frying

6-8 SERVINGS

1. Wash and clean the zucchini well. Dry them with paper towel. Cut them into circles $1/2$ inch thick. Set them aside.
2. Prepare the batter in a deep bowl by mixing the flour, cornstarch, baking powder, salt, and pepper. Add the beer and whisk with a mixer until an even, smooth batter is formed.
3. Pour sufficient oil into a large nonstick skillet and heat the oil over medium heat.
4. When the oil is hot, place about 4 zucchini slices into the batter at one time, and then, with the help of tongs, put the slices into the hot oil. Cook the zucchini until they turn golden on both sides (about $1^{1}/_{2}$ minutes per side). Using clean tongs, remove the cooked beignets (fritters) and drain them on a platter covered with paper towels. Keep warm in the oven until all the slices have been cooked. Cook the rest of the zucchini slices in the same way, adding more oil as needed. Check the seasonings and serve them hot.

# Eggplant Fritters (Beignets d'Aubergines)

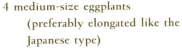

4 medium-size eggplants
  (preferably elongated like the
  Japanese type)
A pinch of salt
2 cups white flour
4 tablespoons cornstarch

1 tablespoon baking powder
White pepper to taste
2 cups cold dark beer
Olive oil (or canola oil), as needed,
  for deep frying

6 SERVINGS

1. Clean and trim the ends of the eggplant. Cut the eggplants in 1/2-inch-thick slices. Place them in a container filled with cold water, add a pinch of salt, and let them stand for 2 hours. Afterward, drain them well, and set them aside.

2. In a deep bowl prepare the batter by mixing the flour, cornstarch, baking powder, salt, and pepper. Add the beer, and whisk with a mixer until an even, smooth batter is formed.

3. Pour sufficient oil into a large nonstick skillet and heat the oil over medium heat.

4. When the oil is hot, place 3 eggplant slices in the batter at one time, and then, with the help of tongs, put the slices into the hot oil. Cook the eggplants until they turn golden on both sides (about 2 minutes per side). Using clean tongs, remove the cooked beignets (fritters) and drain them on a platter covered with paper towels. Keep warm in the oven until all the slices have been cooked. Cook the rest of the eggplant slices in the same way, adding more oil as needed. Check the seasonings and serve them hot.

# Parsnips and Carrots Exupery

1 pound firm parsnips
1 pound carrots
4 cups water
Salt to taste
1 teaspoon sugar
5 tablespoons butter (or margarine),
    more if needed

4 tablespoons maple syrup
A dash of dried mustard
Finely chopped fresh parsley (or
    chervil), as garnish

8 SERVINGS

1. Wash and trim the vegetables. Peel the carrots but do not peel the parsnips. Slice the vegetables in even round circles and place them in a saucepan. Add the water and bring it to a boil. Add the salt and sugar. Reduce the heat to low-medium. Cover the saucepan and simmer gently for 20 minutes.

2. Drain the vegetables. Melt the butter in a saucepan. Add the maple syrup and dried mustard. Mix well with a wooden spatula until the mixture turns into a blended sauce. Add the vegetables and gently toss them until they are well coated with the sauce. Serve them hot with some finely chopped parsley or chervil, as garnish.

# Leek Croûtes in White Wine

## ( POIREAUX EN CROÛTES AU VIN BLANC )

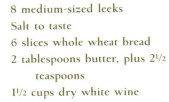

8 medium-sized leeks
Salt to taste
6 slices whole wheat bread
2 tablespoons butter, plus 2½
   teaspoons
1½ cups dry white wine

2 tablespoons cornstarch
Freshly ground black pepper to
   taste
3 tablespoons heavy cream
Finely chopped fresh chives, as
   garnish

6 SERVINGS

1. Preheat the oven to 200°. Clean the leeks well and trim them. Slice them with care 1 inch thick. Place them in a large saucepan, fill with water and add salt, and bring to a boil. Cook in the boiling water for about 10 minutes. Drain and set them aside.

2. Trim off the crusts from the bread slices. Melt about 2½ teaspoons of the butter in a large skillet and brown both sides of the bread slices lightly. Both sides must be evenly coated. Place the slices in an oven-proof dish and keep them warm in the oven.

3. Melt the remaining 2 tablespoons butter in another large skillet. Add ½ cup of the white wine. Dilute well the cornstarch in the remaining 1 cup wine and add to the skillet. Add salt and pepper and stir constantly until a roux is formed. Add the heavy cream and blend well. Add the leeks and toss gently with a wooden spoon. Allow the leeks to reheat.

4. Place one slice of the warm bread on each individual plate. Place even amounts of the leek sauce on the top of each slice. Garnish the top with the finely chopped chives and serve hot. It is an excellent appetizer.

# Eggplant Puree

3 medium-size eggplants, cubed
3 medium-size onions, coarsely
   chopped
6 tablespoons olive oil (or butter)
1½ cups milk, more if needed

Salt and freshly ground black
   pepper to taste
Nutmeg
2 tablespoons butter
Chervil, as garnish

4-6 SERVINGS

1. Place the cubed eggplants and the onions in a good-size nonstick saucepan. Add the oil and sauté briefly over low-medium heat until the eggplants are evenly coated. Stir frequently.

2. Add the milk, salt, pepper, and nutmeg. Stir well and cover the saucepan. Continue cooking over low-medium heat and stir occasionally. Check to see if more milk may be necessary. Cook for about 15–20 minutes, until all the liquid is absorbed. Puree the mixture with a masher and add the butter. Mix well.

3. Serve the puree hot, with finely chopped chervil on the top as garnish.

# Sweet Pea Mousse

*Mayonnaise*

1 egg yolk
1 teaspoon french mustard (Dijon
    or other)
Salt and white pepper to taste

3/4 cup light olive oil
2 teaspoons vinegar (preferably
    tarragon flavor)

3 teaspoons butter
1 cup fresh (or frozen) sweet peas
1 medium-size onion, finely
    chopped
A dash of salt
2/3 cup water
12 ounces cottage cheese

12 ounces ricotta cheese
1/2 cup finely chopped fresh parsley
1 cup homemade mayonnaise (see
    above)
Salt and freshly ground black
    pepper to taste

6-8 SERVINGS

1. To prepare the mayonnaise, place the egg yolk in a deep bowl and add the mustard, salt, and white pepper, and a few drops of the olive oil. Begin to mix with a whisk or a mixer. (I always use a mixer.) Add the remaining oil little by little while continuing to mix. Toward the end add the vinegar and continue mixing until a rich thick consistency is reached. Keep the mayonnaise in the refrigerator until ready to be used.

2. Melt the butter in a saucepan. Add the peas, onion, and salt. Stir well and sauté briefly over low-medium heat for about 2 minutes.

3. After 2 minutes, add 2/3 cup water. Stir again and cover the saucepan. Cook for about 7–8 minutes, until all the liquid is absorbed. Remove from the heat.

4. Into a large bowl place the cottage cheese, ricotta cheese, pea mixture, and parsley and mix well. Add the mayonnaise and blend all ingredients thoroughly. Check the seasonings.

5. Choose a good mold for the mousse, hollow at the center. Cover the bottom part with plastic wrap for better unmolding at the end. Pour the pea-cheese mixture into the mold and gently press it down with a spatula. Smooth the top with the spatula. Place the mousse in the refrigerator for at least 2 hours before serving. Unmold it carefully onto a serving plate. Remove the plastic wrap and serve cold.

# Parsnip Orange Flavor Puree

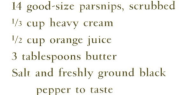

14 good-size parsnips, scrubbed
$^1/_3$ cup heavy cream
$^1/_2$ cup orange juice
3 tablespoons butter
Salt and freshly ground black
    pepper to taste

$^1/_2$ teaspoon nutmeg
Finely chopped fresh parsley, as
    garnish

4-6 SERVINGS

1. Cut the parsnips in thin slices and place them in a large saucepan filled with water. Over medium heat bring the water to a boil, cover the saucepan, and cook the parsnips for about a half hour. Drain and allow to cool.

2. Puree the parsnips evenly with a masher, or pass them through a sieve. Place the pureed parsnips back into the saucepan. Add the heavy cream and orange juice. Cook over low-medium heat, stirring constantly until most of the liquid is absorbed by the puree.

3. Add the butter, salt, pepper, and nutmeg. Blend the ingredients well and serve hot. If you prepare it ahead of time, butter thoroughly an ovenproof dish, put the puree into it, and keep it warm in a preheated 200° oven until ready to serve. Just before serving sprinkle some finely chopped parsley on the top as garnish.

# Belgian Endives in Béchamel Sauce

6 medium-size Belgian endives,
    trimmed
1 large onion, coarsely chopped

A dash of sea salt and white pepper
1/2 cup dry white wine

*Béchamel Sauce*

3 tablespoons butter (or olive oil)
3 teaspoons cornstarch
    (or 2 tablespoons flour)
1 1/2 cups milk
Salt and freshly ground black
    pepper to taste

A dash of nutmeg
1 cup grated Emmental cheese
    (or Swiss cheese)

6 SERVINGS

1. Melt butter in a large nonstick skillet. Add the endives and onion. Sauté over medium heat, turning the endives until they are brown on all sides. Add salt and pepper. Add the wine, cover the pot, and reduce the heat to low-medium. Simmer for about 25–30 minutes until the liquid has evaporated. Remove the skillet from the heat.

2. Preheat the oven to 350°.

3. Prepare a quick béchamel by melting the butter over low-medium heat in a nonstick saucepan. Dilute the cornstarch or flour in the milk and add the mixture gradually to the melted butter. Stir continually. Add the salt, pepper, and nutmeg and continue stirring until a thick consistency is reached.

4. Butter an ovenproof dish. Pour in half the béchamel and run it over the bottom of the dish. Arrange the endives and the onion, spread evenly, on top of the béchamel. Pour the remaining béchamel on top of the vegetables. Sprinkle the grated cheese evenly over the top.

5. Place the dish in the oven for 30 minutes. The dish is done when the top turns brown and bubbly. Serve hot.

# Fava Beans and Potato Puree

3 cups precooked fava beans (or
  three 15-ounce cans, drained)
3 large potatoes, cooked and cut
  into quarters
2 tablespoons butter, plus 2
  teaspoons

1 onion, finely chopped
A few sage leaves, crumbled
Salt and freshly ground black
  pepper to taste
1/2 cup heavy cream

4 SERVINGS

1. Place the fava beans and the potatoes, all precooked, in a large saucepan and puree them coarsely with a masher. Create a smooth consistency.
2. Melt the 2 tablespoons butter in another saucepan and add the onion and sage. Sauté lightly over low-medium heat until the onions begin to turn translucent. Sprinkle on the salt and pepper, and add the cream. Mix ingredients well.
3. Immediately, add the fava-potato mixture and continue stirring until a rich well-blended consistency is achieved. Add the remaining 2 teaspoons butter and stir some more. Serve the puree hot.

# "Les Pyrénées" Stuffed Tomatoes

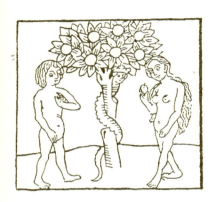

4 good-size ripe tomatoes
4 hard-boiled eggs, coarsely
   chopped
1 small onion, finely chopped
6 pitted black olives, finely
   chopped
3 tablespoons small capers

5 tablespoons finely chopped fresh
   parsley (save some for garnish)
5 tablespoons mayonnaise,
   homemade or commercial
1 teaspoon lemon juice
Salt and freshly ground black
   pepper to taste
8 lettuce leaves

4 SERVINGS

1. Wash and clean the tomatoes well. With a sharp knife slice them across the very top and carefully scoop out their insides. Place them upside down on a paper towel, to drain their remaining juice.

2. Place the chopped, hard-boiled eggs in a deep bowl. Add the onion, olives, capers, parsley, mayonnaise, lemon juice, salt, and pepper. Mix the ingredients well and keep refrigerated until ready to serve.

3. When ready to serve, place 2 flat lettuce leaves on each plate. Put the tomato on the lettuce leaves. Fill each tomato to the very top with the egg mixture. Sprinkle some finely chopped parsley over the tomatoes and serve cold. It is an excellent summer appetizer.

# Riviera Stuffed Tomatoes

6 medium-size ripe tomatoes
14 ounces goat cheese
8 tablespoons virgin olive oil
2 tablespoons finely chopped fresh
     basil (or 1 tablespoon dried)
2 teaspoons finely chopped fresh
     thyme (or 1 teaspoon dried)

2 teaspoons finely chopped fresh
     rosemary (or 1 teaspoon dried)
1 garlic clove, finely minced
Salt and freshly ground black
     pepper to taste
8 teaspoons bread crumbs

*Sauce*

3 tablespoons olive oil
1 onion, finely chopped
Tomato insides, chopped (see above)
2 tablespoons finely chopped fresh
     basil

Salt and freshly ground black
     pepper to taste
1–2 tomatoes, peeled and chopped,
     if needed

4-6 SERVINGS

1.  Preheat the oven to 350°. Carefully slice off the tops of the tomatoes and hollow out the insides. Reserve the pulp for the sauce. The tomato shells must remain intact. Place them upside down on a plate covered with a paper towel to drain their remaining liquid.

2.  In a deep bowl mash the goat cheese with a fork. Add the oil, basil, thyme, rosemary, garlic, salt, pepper, and bread crumbs. Mix the ingredients well. Fill each tomato shell with the goat mixture.

3.  Place the stuffed tomatoes in a well-buttered flat baking dish. Bake for about 25–30 minutes.

4.  While the tomatoes are baking, make a quick tomato sauce by pouring the oil into a nonstick saucepan. Add the onion, insides of the tomatoes, basil, salt, and pepper, and cook over low-medium heat, stirring frequently, until a nice sauce is achieved. Make sure it does not dry. If

need be, add more peeled chopped tomatoes ( 1 or 2 ). When the sauce is done, turn off the heat, and cover the saucepan.

5. When the tomatoes are baked, remove them from the oven and place them in individual serving dishes. Reheat the sauce briefly and pour some over each tomato top. Serve immediately. Serve hot.

# Easy Spinach Croquettes

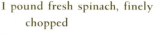

1 pound fresh spinach, finely
    chopped
7 eggs, beaten
2 tablespoons milk
2 garlic cloves, finely minced

2 cups bread crumbs
1 cup grated Parmesan cheese
Salt and freshly ground black
    pepper to taste

8-10 SERVINGS

1. Boil the spinach in salted water until well cooked. Drain thoroughly, squeezing all the water out of it.
2. Beat the eggs in a deep bowl. Add the milk and beat some more. Add the garlic, bread crumbs, cheese, salt, and pepper. Add the spinach and mix the ingredients well. Place the bowl in the refrigerator for at least 2 hours, or ready to use.
3. Preheat the oven to 350°. Butter thoroughly one or two ovenproof dishes. Moisten your hands with water and shape the spinach mixture into balls (about 1 1/2 inches) by rolling them carefully with both hands.
4. Carefully place the croquettes into the baking dishes, leaving some space in between. Bake for about 25–30 minutes. Serve them warm.

# Zucchini Ratatouille

¼ cup virgin olive oil
2 onions, chopped
6 tomatoes, peeled and coarsely
    chopped
3 garlic cloves, minced
4 medium zucchini, sliced

1 bay leaf
½ teaspoon chopped fresh oregano
    (or ¼ teaspoon dried)
Salt and freshly ground black
    pepper to taste

6-8 SERVINGS

1. Pour the oil in a large nonstick pot. Add the onions and sauté briefly over low-medium heat. Add the tomatoes and garlic. Stir. Cover the pot and cook for about 15 minutes.

2. Add the zucchini, bay leaf, oregano, salt, and pepper. Stir gently for a couple of minutes. Then cover the pot and continue cooking over low-medium heat for another 20–30 minutes. Stir occasionally. Remove the bay leaf. Serve hot.

# Eggplant Steaks with Red Pepper Sauce

3 large eggplants, cut into ½-inch
   slices

1 tablespoon salt
Olive oil, as needed

*Sauce*

4 sweet red peppers, roasted,
   seeded, peeled, and sliced in
   even quarters
4 garlic cloves, roasted, peeled, and
   minced
⅓ cup fresh basil leaves, chopped

1 tablespoon lemon juice
1 teaspoon Dijon mustard
Salt and freshly ground black
   pepper to taste
1 cup heavy cream

6 SERVINGS

1. Cover a long dish (or dishes) with paper towel(s). Spread the eggplant slices over it. Sprinkle them with salt and let them stand for
   1½ hours. At the end of the process, dry them with clean paper towels.

2. Preheat the oven to 200°. Heat oil to medium in a large iron, nonstick
   skillet. Add several eggplant slices at a time, and cook them until they
   darken on both sides. When they are done, place them in an ovenproof dish, cover with foil, and keep them warm in the oven. Repeat
   with the remaining eggplant slices, adding more oil as needed.

3. Prepare the sauce by placing the roasted peppers, garlic, basil, lemon
   juice, mustard, salt, and pepper in a food processor. Mix and blend
   the ingredients well.

4. Heat the heavy cream in a nonstick saucepan over low-medium heat.
   Add the pepper mixture gradually, and stir continually until sauce is
   thick and smooth.

5. When ready to serve, place 2 or 3 eggplant slices on each plate, and
   pour some sauce on top of the eggplants. Serve hot.

# Sorrel-Potato Puree

2 potatoes, peeled and sliced into
    chunks
1/3 cup milk
3 tablespoons butter
1 1/2 tablespoons trimmed and
    chopped fresh sorrel leaves

Salt and freshly ground black
    pepper to taste
1/2 teaspoon nutmeg
6 tablespoons heavy cream (or
    crème fraîche)

4 SERVINGS

1. Boil the potatoes in salted water until tender. Drain the water and put the potatoes back in the saucepan. Mash them thoroughly. Add the milk and mix well over low-medium heat until smooth. Turn off the heat.

2. Melt the butter in a nonstick saucepan. Add the sorrel, salt, pepper, and nutmeg, and cook over low-medium heat, stirring continually until the mixture turns into a thick and even sauce. Add the potato mixture and heavy cream, and continue stirring until all the liquid evaporates and a rich, thick puree is formed. Serve hot, as an accompaniment to fish or egg main courses.

# Potato and Escarole Puree (Puree Verte)

1 pound potatoes, peeled and cubed
1 head escarole, coarsely chopped
1 bunch of watercress, coarsely
    chopped
4 tablespoons half-and-half

3 tablespoons butter
3 garlic cloves, peeled and minced
Salt and freshly ground black
    pepper to taste

4-6 SERVINGS

1. Boil the potatoes for about 15–20 minutes. (Add a pinch of salt at will.) Drain.
2. Boil the escarole and watercress for about 10 minutes. Drain and save 1/2 cup of the cooking liquid.
3. Using a food processor, mix well and puree the potatoes, escarole, and watercress.
4. Pour the 1/2 cup of cooking liquid saved from boiling the greens into a casserole, add the puree, and keep it warm over low heat. Add the half-and-half and mix well.
5. Melt the butter over low-medium heat in a small skillet, add the minced garlic, stir a few times, and then add it to the puree. Add the salt and pepper and mix the ingredients well. Serve the puree warm, as an accompaniment to fish, fowl, or egg dishes.

# Potato, Leek, and Carrot Puree

6 large potatoes, peeled and cubed
3 leeks, trimmed and sliced, using
    the lower part of the greens
3 long thin carrots, peeled and
    thinly sliced

5 tablespoons heavy cream
3 tablespoons butter
A dash of nutmeg
Salt and freshly ground black
    pepper to taste

6 SERVINGS

1. Boil the vegetables in water to cover for about 20–25 minutes. You may add a pinch of salt toward the end of the boiling, but just a tiny bit. Drain the vegetables and save the cooking liquid.

2. Process the vegetables in a food processor until a puree consistency is achieved.

3. Pour $1/2$ cup of the cooking liquid (the rest can be saved as vegetable stock for soups or for another use) into a casserole, add the pureed vegetables, and keep them warm over low heat. Add the cream, stir and mix well.

4. Melt the butter at low-medium heat in a small skillet and stir into the puree. Add the nutmeg, salt, and pepper. Blend the ingredients well and serve the puree as an accompaniment to a main course.

MUSHROOMS

# Herbs and Almond-Stuffed Mushrooms

12 large mushrooms
18 tablespoons olive oil
1 tablespoon lemon juice
Salt and freshly ground black
　　pepper to taste
8 tablespoons milk
6 tablespoons olive oil
1 egg, beaten
2 garlic cloves, minced
2/3 cup bread crumbs

1/4 cup almonds, chopped
1 tablespoon chopped fresh
　　rosemary (or 1/2 tablespoon
　　dried)
2 tablespoons chopped fresh thyme
　　(or 1 tablespoon dried)
1/3 cup chopped fresh parsley
2 tablespoons chopped fresh chives
　　(or 1 tablespoon dried)
Rind of 1 small lemon, finely
　　chopped

4 SERVINGS

1. Preheat the oven to 350°.

2. Clean and dry the mushrooms with paper towels. Remove the stems and chop them finely. Place them in a bowl, add 12 tablespoons of the olive oil, the lemon juice, salt, and pepper. Mix the ingredients well and set the bowl aside. Set the the mushroom caps aside.

3. Into a separate bowl, pour the milk, the remaining 6 tablespoons olive oil, and the beaten egg. Add the garlic, bread crumbs, chopped almonds, all the herbs, and the lemon rind. Mix the ingredients well. Add the contents of the other bowl, check the seasonings, and mix thoroughly.

4. Spoon the mixture into the mushroom caps. Place the mushrooms in a well-buttered ovenproof dish and bake for about 20–25 minutes. Remove them from the oven, allow them to cool for a few minutes, and then serve at room temperature.

NOTE: The stuffed mushrooms can be served separately on a tray before dinner, or as hors d'oeuvre or appetizer at the table. In this latter case serve 3 mushrooms per person.

# Porcini Mushrooms au Gratin

2 tablespoons butter
4 shallots, finely chopped
1 pound fresh porcini mushrooms,
    trimmed
Salt to taste

1 tablespoon lemon juice
1/2 cup heavy cream
3 tablespoons Calvados liqueur
Grated Parmesan cheese, as needed

4-6 SERVINGS

1. Preheat the oven to 300°.
2. Melt the butter in a large nonstick skillet. Add the shallots and sauté gently over low-medium heat.
3. Remove the stems from the mushrooms. Wipe them clean with a paper towel. Chop them coarsely. Wipe the mushroom caps clean and slice them in halves.
4. Add the mushroom caps and stems, the salt, and the lemon juice to the shallots and continue cooking over low-medium heat for about 8–10 minutes. Cover the skillet, but stir occasionally.
5. After 10 minutes add the heavy cream and the Calvados. Stir well and continue cooking for another 3–5 minutes.
6. Butter thoroughly an ovenproof dish. Place the mushroom mixture in it and distribute it evenly over the dish. Sprinkle the Parmesan cheese over the top and place the dish in the oven for about 15 minutes. Serve hot.

# Spinach with Portobello Mushrooms

FOR ME, PRAYER MEANS THE

LAUNCHING OUT OF THE HEART

TOWARDS GOD; IT MEANS LIFTING UP

ONE'S EYES, IN SIMPLICITY, TO

HEAVEN, A CRY OF GRATEFUL LOVE.

ST. THÉRÈSE OF LISIEUX

1 pound fresh spinach, washed and
    trimmed
8 portobello mushrooms, trimmed
    and sliced
1 large Vidalia onion, sliced
    (or Spanish onion)

8 tablespoons extra-virgin olive oil,
    more if needed
Salt and freshly ground black
    pepper to taste
A dash of nutmeg

6 SERVINGS

1. Place the spinach in a saucepan filled with water. Bring to a boil, lower the heat to medium, cover the saucepan, and simmer gently for about a half hour. Drain thoroughly.

2. While the spinach is cooking, place the mushrooms and onion in a large nonstick skillet. Add the oil, sauté over low-medium heat for about 8–10 minutes until the onion turns golden. Stir frequently, and add more oil if necessary.

3. When the onions turn golden, add the spinach, salt, pepper, and nutmeg. Stir frequently until all the ingredients are well blended. Check the seasonings and serve hot. This is an excellent accompaniment to a fish, meat, or egg main course.

# Mushroom Croûtes (Champignons en Croûtes)

4 slices whole wheat bread
5 shallots
16 mushrooms
2 tablespoons butter, plus 2
    teaspoons, more if needed
Salt and freshly ground black
    pepper to taste

3 tablespoons dry white wine
1/2 cup heavy cream
Optional: finely chopped fresh
    chervil (or fresh parsley), as
    garnish

4 SERVINGS

1. Preheat the oven to 200°. Trim off the crusts from the bread slices. Discard the crusts and set the slices aside.
2. Peel and chop the shallots coarsely. Trim the stems from the mushrooms and discard. Clean and wipe the caps. Slice them.
3. Melt 2 teaspoons of the butter in a large skillet and brown the 4 slices of bread on both sides. Once the slices are evenly coated on both sides, place them on an ovenproof plate and keep them warm in the oven.
4. Melt 2 tablespoons of the butter in the same (clean) or separate skillet. Add the shallots, mushrooms, salt, pepper, and wine, and sauté over low-medium heat until the mushrooms are cooked. Stir often. Add the cream and continue stirring until a well-blended sauce is achieved.
5. Place 1 slice of bread on each plate. Distribute and arrange evenly the mushroom sauce on top of each slice and serve hot.

NOTE: This can be served as a side dish to the main course, or as an appetizer.

# Portobellos in Port Sauce

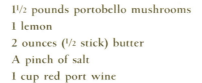

1½ pounds portobello mushrooms
1 lemon
2 ounces (½ stick) butter
A pinch of salt
1 cup red port wine

5 tablespoons heavy cream
1 egg yolk, beaten
Freshly ground black pepper to
   taste

4-6 SERVINGS

1. Cut the stems off the mushrooms (and use them for another purpose).
   Clean the caps with a wet cloth.
2. Pour all the juice from 1 lemon into a container filled with cold water.
   Add the mushrooms and let them stand for a half hour. Drain them
   thoroughly and slice them in halves.
3. Preheat the oven to 350°. Melt the butter in a large nonstick skillet
   and keep it heated over medium heat. Add the mushrooms and salt,
   and sauté them for 10–12 minutes, while stirring frequently.
4. Mix the port and heavy cream in a saucepan. Stir and bring to a quick
   boil. Remove from the heat, allow to cool a bit, and whisk in the egg
   yolk. Add some salt and pepper, and blend the ingredients well.
5. Butter thoroughly an ovenproof dish. Spread the mushrooms evenly
   in the dish. Pour the sauce over the mushrooms. Place the dish in the
   oven for 10–15 minutes maximum. Serve them hot.

NOTE: This can be served as a side dish to the main course, or as an
appetizer for an elegant dinner.

# St. Cuthbert Potato and Mushroom Stew

1 pound Idaho potatoes, peeled and
    cut into 1-inch cubes
8 tablespoons olive oil
1 pound fresh mushrooms, cleaned,
    trimmed, and halved
1 large onion, chopped

1 cup dry white wine
1/2 teaspoon cornstarch
2 bay leaves
A pinch of salt and freshly ground
    black pepper

6-8 SERVINGS

1. Cook the potatoes in boiling salted water for about 3 minutes. Drain them completely and set them aside.

2. Pour the oil into a nonstick casserole set over medium-high heat. Add the mushrooms and the onion, and sauté briefly for 2 minutes. Lower the heat to low and add 1/2 cup of the wine. Cover the casserole and simmer for 15 minutes.

3. Dilute the cornstarch in the remaining 1/2 cup wine and add it to the casserole. Add the bay leaves, drained potatoes, salt, and pepper, and stir well. (If all the wine is absorbed, add more.) Cover the casserole and continue simmering for another 15–20 minutes, until the vegetables are tender and the mixture has turned into a stew. Stir well, remove the bay leaves, and serve as an accompaniment to fish, egg, or meat main courses.

# Mushrooms à la Bordelaise

## ( CÈPES À LA BORDELAISE )

2 pounds mushrooms
4 tablespoons lemon juice
A pinch of salt
1/2 cup olive oil
1/2 cup dry white Bordeaux wine
4 shallots, minced

3 garlic cloves, peeled and minced
Freshly ground black pepper to
taste
Finely chopped fresh parsley, as
garnish

4-6 SERVINGS

1. Wash and dry the mushrooms. Separate the stems and the caps. Place the caps (or hats) in a big bowl and pour on the lemon juice. Add the salt. Mix well and let the mushrooms stand for 1 hour or so. Set the stems aside.

2. Pour half the olive oil into a large nonstick skillet set over medium-high heat. When the oil is hot, add the mushrooms caps and sauté one side of the mushrooms for about 2 minutes. Turn and sauté the other side for another 2 minutes. Lower the heat to low and add the wine. Cover the skillet and simmer gently for about 30 minutes. Stir occasionally.

3. Chop the stems finely and place them in a separate skillet. Add the remaining 1/4 cup oil, the shallots, garlic, salt, and pepper, and sauté briefly over low-medium heat for about 2 minutes. Stir frequently.

4. Just before serving, add the stem-shallot mixture to the rest of the mushrooms and mix well. Check the seasonings, sprinkle the parsley on the top, as garnish, and serve hot. This is an excellent accompaniment to any main course.

# St. Seraphim's Mushroom Sauce

1 ounce (¹/4 stick) butter (or
    margarine)
3 shallots, finely chopped
¹/2 pound fresh mushrooms,
    cleaned, trimmed, and sliced

1 cup dry sherry or dry white wine
¹/2 teaspoon ground turmeric
Salt and freshly ground black
    pepper to taste
¹/2 cup finely chopped fresh parsley

MAKES 1¹/4 CUPS

Melt the butter in an enamel or stainless steel saucepan. Add the shallots, mushrooms, turmeric, salt, and pepper and cook over medium
heat for a few minutes until the mushrooms begin to turn brown. Add
the sherry or wine and reduce the heat. Add the parsley while stirring
continuously. Cook thoroughly for another 5–6 minutes until the
sauce is achieved.

NOTE: This sauce is excellent on the top of rice, fish, meat, and eggs.

# Mushrooms à la Barigoule

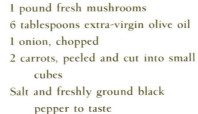

1 pound fresh mushrooms
6 tablespoons extra-virgin olive oil
1 onion, chopped
2 carrots, peeled and cut into small
    cubes
Salt and freshly ground black
    pepper to taste

1 cup dry white wine
3 garlic cloves, peeled and minced
5 tablespoons water
Chopped fresh parsley, as garnish

4-6 SERVINGS

1. Clean well and trim the mushrooms. At the center slice them in half lengthwise.
2. Pour the oil into a nonstick casserole (if possible cast-iron). Add the onion and carrots. Place the mushrooms on the top. Sprinkle with salt and pepper. Cover the casserole and cook over low-medium heat for about 3–4 minutes. Stir frequently.
3. Remove the lid add the wine, garlic, and water. Stir well and reduce the heat to low. Re-cover the casserole and continue cooking for 15 minutes more. Remove the lid again and cook for another 5 minutes until the liquid is reduced to one third or less its original amount. Check the seasonings, sprinkle some freshly chopped parsley on the top as garnish, and serve as an accompaniment to the main course.

9

FISH

# Red Snapper Marinière

4 tablespoons olive oil
4 red snapper fillets, about 8
    ounces each
3 tablespoons finely chopped fresh
    parsley
A pinch of fresh thyme
3 shallots, finely chopped

Salt and freshly ground black
    pepper to taste
1 cup dry white wine, more if
    needed
4 teaspoons butter
Finely chopped fresh chervil, as
    garnish

4 SERVINGS

1. Heat the oil in a good-size skillet. Add the snapper fillets and cook over low-medium heat for 2 minutes. Turn the fillets over.

2. Add the parsley, thyme, shallots, salt, pepper, and the wine. Bring the liquid to a boil. Keep the low-medium heat, cover the skillet, and continue cooking for another 8 minutes. (If the wine evaporates, add a few tablespoons extra to keep the moisture in the skillet.)

3. When the fillets are cooked and most of the liquid has evaporated, dot 1 teaspoon butter on the top of each fillet. Cover the skillet for a half minute. Serve immediately, accompanying each fillet with some of the sauce, and topping each with the finely chopped chervil.

# Fish Côte d'Azur Style

4 tablespoons extra-virgin olive oil
6 fish fillets
2 shallots, chopped
6 tomatoes, peeled and quartered
A pinch of fresh rosemary
A pinch of thyme (fresh or dried)
1 bay leaf

3 garlic cloves, minced
18 pitted black olives (3 per person)
Salt and white pepper to taste
1/2 cup dry white wine
4 tablespoons lemon juice
Thin lemon slices, as garnish

6 SERVINGS

1. Pour the oil into a large nonstick skillet, and add the fish fillets. Add also the shallots, tomatoes, rosemary, thyme, bay leaf, and minced garlic. Cover the skillet and cook for a few minutes over low-medium heat. Turn the fillets over at least once.

2. Add the olives, salt, pepper, wine, and lemon juice. Raise the heat to medium and bring the mixture to a boil. Re-cover the skillet and simmer gently for 12–15 minutes until most of the liquid is absorbed. Carefully turn the fillets over once or twice. Serve the fish hot or cold. Pour some of the sauce on the top of each fillet, and garnish them with the thin slices of lemon.

# Rodez Codfish with Potatoes (L'Estonfinado)

2 pounds dried salt cod
2 cups dry white wine
8 new potatoes
4 eggs
4 garlic cloves, finely chopped

8 sprigs of parsley, finely chopped
Salt and freshly ground pepper to
    taste
1/2 cup extra-virgin olive oil

6-8 SERVINGS

1. Soak the fish overnight in cold water. The following day, drain the water and place the cod in a casserole. Add the wine and simmer over low-medium heat for about 30 minutes, covered. Drain the cod, then immediately remove the skin and bones. Shred the cod, using two forks.

2. While the cod is slowly cooking, peel and slice the potatoes. Boil them in salted water for about 25 minutes. Drain and mash them thoroughly.

3. Preheat the oven to 350°. Beat the eggs in a deep bowl. Add the shredded cod, mashed potatoes, garlic, parsley, salt, and pepper, and mix the ingredients until well blended.

4. Use some of the oil to thoroughly grease a long baking dish, and place the cod mixture in it. Spread evenly. Pour the remaining oil over the whole surface. Bake for 20 minutes. Serve hot.

# Deauville Shrimp Bisque

2 tablespoons butter
1/2 pound shrimp, shelled and
    deveined
2 shallots, finely chopped
1/4 cup brandy (or Calvados)
2 1/2 cups dry white wine
2 1/2 cups water

1 bay leaf
A pinch of dried thyme
Salt and freshly ground black
    pepper to taste
3 hard-boiled eggs, crumbled
4 tablespoons tomato paste
1/2 teaspoon paprika

4-6 SERVINGS

1. Heat the butter in a good-size cast-iron saucepan. Add the shrimp and shallots and sauté lightly over medium heat for 4–5 minutes. Stir frequently. Add the brandy or Calvados and ignite it. Being very careful, stir with long metal spoon and let the flames die out.

2. Add the wine, water, bay leaf, thyme, salt, and pepper and bring the bisque to a boil. Cover the saucepan, reduce the heat to low-medium, and simmer for 15–20 minutes. Remove the shrimp and set aside. Remove and discard the bay leaf.

3. In a deep bowl mash well the shrimp and eggs. Add 2/3 cup of the liquid in the pan. Add the tomato paste and paprika. Mix the ingredients well and return the mixture to the saucepan. Reheat, stir well, and check the seasonings. Serve the bisque hot.

# Salmon Mousse in a Spinach Bed

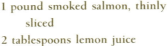

1 pound smoked salmon, thinly
    sliced
2 tablespoons lemon juice
2 eggs
3/4 cup half-and-half

1 teaspoon finely grated lemon rind
Salt and freshly ground black
    pepper to taste
Butter, as needed
24 fresh spinach leaves, trimmed

*Sauce*

2 tablespoons butter
2 teaspoons cornstarch
    (or 4 teaspoons flour)
1/2 cup milk
1/2 cup dry white wine

Salt and freshly ground black
    pepper to taste
2 egg yolks, well beaten
1/2 teaspoon finely grated lemon
    rind

4 SERVINGS

1. Preheat the oven to 350°. Place the salmon slices in a blender. Add the lemon juice, eggs, half-and-half, lemon rind, salt, and pepper, and whirl until the ingredients are well blended.

2. Butter thoroughly four ramekins and fill them with the salmon mixture, pressing it down with a small spatula. Place the ramekins in a pan large enough to hold all of them and fill the pan with water up to half the height of the ramekins. Place the pan in the oven for about 20–25 minutes, or until the blade of a thin knife inserted in the center of a ramekin comes out clean. (Do not overcook!)

3. Wash and clean the spinach leaves well. Drain and dry them. Place the leaves on each individual dish in the form of a star, with the former stem area toward the center of the plate.

4. While baking the mousse, prepare a quick fish sauce by melting the butter in a nonstick saucepan. Dilute the cornstarch in the milk and add gradually to the butter, over low-medium heat, while stirring

continuously. Add the wine, salt, and pepper and continue to stir until the sauce thickens. Remove it from the heat. Stir in the egg yolks and grated lemon rind gradually, whisking fast until the sauce is even and smooth. It must be done quickly so that the eggs don't cook in the sauce. Reheat it before serving.

5. When the mousse is done, unmold it carefully over the spinach, in the center of the plate. Pour the sauce over the mousse and the spinach. Serve it warm.

# Salmon Fillets St. Celestine

RESPECTABILITY AND SECURITY ARE

SUBTLE TRAPS ON LIFE'S JOURNEY.

THOSE WHO ARE DRAWN TO EXTREMES

ARE OFTEN NEARER TO RENEWAL AND

SELF-DISCOVERY. THOSE TRAPPED IN

THE BLAND MIDDLE REGION OF

RESPECTABILITY ARE LOST WITHOUT

EVER REALIZING IT.

JOHN O'DONOHUE, ANAM CARA

3 leeks
12 mushrooms
3 tablespoons butter (or 4
    tablespoons olive oil)
4 salmon fillets
Salt and freshly ground black
    pepper to taste

2 cups dry white wine, more if
    needed
6 tablespoons heavy cream
2 egg yolks, well beaten
A bunch of sorrel leaves, finely
    chopped

4 SERVINGS

1. Wash and trim the leeks. Slice them 1 inch long up to within 1 inch of the green part. Wash, trim, and slice the mushrooms.

2. Melt the butter over low-medium heat in a large nonstick skillet, and add the leeks and mushrooms. Place the salmon fillets on top. Sprinkle some salt and freshly ground pepper over them. Pour the wine all around the fillets. Cover the skillet and cook over low-medium heat for about 20 minutes, adding more wine, if needed. Turn over the fillets, at least once, during the cooking.

3. While the fillets are cooking, prepare the sauce by placing the cream and egg yolks in a deep bowl. Beat them with a mixer until an even consistency is achieved. Pour this mixture into a small casserole and heat it over low-medium heat. Stir continually and slowly. Add the sorrel and continue to stir.

4. When the fillets are cooked and are ready to be served, turn them over once more. Pour over them part of the egg-sorrel sauce and cover the skillet. Continue cooking for another 2 minutes or so.

5. Serve the fillets on a bed of leeks and mushrooms, with the remaining sorrel sauce on the top. Serve hot.

# Grilled Sea Bass with Dill Sauce

Olive oil, as needed
2 sea bass fillets (with skin on)

Salt and freshly ground black
    pepper to taste

*Sauce*

1/3 cup chopped fresh dill
5 teaspoons capers
1/2 teaspoon grated lemon peel

1/2 cup heavy cream
A pinch of cayenne pepper
6 tablespoons hot melted butter

4 SERVINGS

1. To prepare the grill, preheat it to very hot. Brush a bit of oil on the grill. With a brush lightly oil the 2 sea bass fillets and season them with salt and pepper. Place the fillets on the grill skin side up. Cook them for about 5–6 minutes, taking acre to avoid burning. When one side is cooked, carefully turn them over and cook the fillets for another 5–6 minutes. Test the fillets to make sure they are cooked through and tender.
2. When fillets are done, place them on a cutting board and remove the skin. Slice each fillet into two equal parts to give exactly four portions.
3. To prepare the sauce, place all the ingredients, except the hot butter, in a blender and whirl. At the last minute, while the blender is still running, slowly pour in the hot butter and blend well.
4. Serve the fillets in warm serving plates, accompanied by the sauce in a small bowl or sauceboat.

SALADS

# Lentil and Celery Heart Salad

2 carrots, peeled and cubed
1/2 pound lentils
1 celery heart, thinly sliced
1 small red onion, finely chopped
1 medium cucumber, peeled,
   seeded, and diced

7 tablespoons olive oil
6 teaspoons lemon juice
Salt and freshly ground black
   pepper to taste
Several sprigs of parsley finely
   minced, as garnish

4-6 SERVINGS

1. Bring water to boil in a good-size saucepan. Add the carrots and lentils and cook gently over medium heat for about 30 minutes. Drain and allow the vegetables to cool.

2. Place the carrots and lentils in a large salad bowl. Add the celery heart, red onion, and the cucumber. Toss the ingredients gently and place the bowl in a refrigerator until ready to use.

3. Just before serving, prepare the vinaigrette by mixing the oil, lemon juice, salt, and pepper. Pour the vinaigrette over the salad and toss it carefully, watching to see that all the ingredients are thoroughly coated. Serve the salad cool, and sprinkle the top with finely minced parsley as garnish.

# Tuscan Salad (PANZANELLA)

5 cups cubed stale country bread

8 pounds ripe pepper tomatoes, cored and cubed

1 red onion, finely chopped

1 medium cucumber, peeled, seeded, and diced

8 black olives, pitted and chopped

6 green olives, pitted and chopped

1/2 cup fresh basil leaves, cut into strips

1 tablespoon fresh thyme leaves (or dried)

6 tablespoons extra-virgin olive oil

3 tablespoons red wine vinegar

Salt and freshly ground black pepper to taste

6-8 SERVINGS

1. Place the bread, the tomatoes, onion, cucumber, and olives in a good-size salad bowl. Add the basil and thyme.

2. Prepare a vinaigrette by mixing well the oil, vinegar, salt, and pepper. Pour the vinaigrette slowly over the salad and toss gently. Set the salad aside, but not in the refrigerator, for about a half hour until the bread cubes soften. Just before serving, check the seasonings and adjust accordingly. This salad should be kept and served at room temperature.

# Zucchini Salad Basque Style

SPRINGTIME IN THE SOUL CAN BE

BEAUTIFUL, HOPEFUL, AND

STRENGTHENING. YOU CAN MAKE

DIFFICULT TRANSITIONS VERY

NATURALLY IN AN UNFORCED AND

SPONTANEOUS WAY.

JOHN O'DONOHUE, ANAM CARA

3 medium zucchini, cubed
4 medium ripe tomatoes, peeled
   and chopped
1 large sweet red pepper, cubed
1 red onion, chopped
7 tablespoons extra-virgin olive oil

3 tablespoons wine vinegar
Salt and freshly ground black
   pepper to taste
Finely chopped fresh parsley, as
   garnish

6-8 SERVINGS

1. Wash the zucchini well and slice into even cubes. Place the zucchini in a large saucepan, add sufficient water, and bring it to a boil. Boil for about 3 minutes. Drain and rinse the zucchini under cold water. Set the zucchini aside.
2. Place the chopped tomatoes, cubed pepper, and chopped onion in a salad bowl. Add the zucchini.
3. Prepare a vinaigrette by mixing well the oil, vinegar, salt, and pepper. Just before serving pour the vinaigrette over the vegetables and toss them gently until they are well coated. Sprinkle the finely chopped parsley on the top and serve.

# Apple, Endive, and Celery Root Salad

4 ripe Golden Delicious apples
1 Belgian endive, thinly sliced
4 tablespoons raisins
Salt and freshly ground black
    pepper to taste
1 tablespoon sugar

7 tablespoons sesame oil (or other
    vegetable oil)
3 tablespoons cider vinegar
2$\frac{1}{2}$ cups shredded celery root
3 tablespoons low-fat mayonnaise
2 tablespoons lemon juice
Lettuce leaves

4-6 SERVINGS

1. Peel and cut the apples into thin slices. Remove the seeds and place the apples on a plate. Add the endive slices and the raisins. Just before serving, prepare a vinaigrette by mixing well in a deep bowl the salt, pepper, sugar, oil, and vinegar. Combine apple mixture and vinaigrette. Toss it.

2. Place the shredded celery root in a separate bowl and add the mayonnaise, lemon juice, salt, and pepper. Mix the ingredients well and place the salad in the refrigerator for about 1–2 hours before serving.

3. When ready to serve, place 1 or 2 (depending on size) lettuce leaves in the center of each plate. Place on half the lettuce leaf a mound of the apple mixture, and on the other half a mound of the celery root salad. Serve immediately, for this salad must be served cold.

# Hudson Valley Salad

SEEK GOD, AND NOT WHERE HE

DWELLS.

ABBA SISOES

1 fennel bulb
5 ripe plum tomatoes
1 red onion, thinly sliced
1 cucumber, peeled and diced
2 ripe avocados
1 garlic clove, minced
1 tablespoon honey mustard

6 tablespoons extra-virgin olive oil
3 teaspoons fresh lemon juice
3 tablespoons finely chopped fresh
cilantro
Salt and freshly ground black
pepper to taste

6 SERVINGS

1. Trim off the top of the fennel bulb, and discard the large tough outer parts. Cut the fennel lengthwise into thin slices. Place the slices in a saucepan filled with water. Boil for about 5 minutes. Drain the fennel under cold water and set it apart.

2. Trim the top of the tomatoes and cut them into small wedges. Place them in a deep salad bowl. Add the fennel, onion, and cucumber.

3. Peel the avocados, cut them in halves, and discard the pits. Slice the avocados in cubes and add them to the salad bowl.

4. Place the garlic, honey mustard, olive oil, lemon juice, cilantro, salt, and pepper in a small bowl. Whisk thoroughly and pour over the salad. Toss the salad gently, and serve immediately.

# Provençal Mesclun Salad with
# Goat Cheese (SALADE DE MESCLUN AVEC DE CHÈVRE)

1 pound tender mixed salad greens
  (mesclun)
1 small red onion, thinly sliced
6 slices goat cheese

6 sprigs of rosemary (or thyme)
Extra-virgin olive oil, as needed
6 slices french bread

*Salad Dressing (Vinaigrette)*

8 tablespoons olive oil
3 tablespoons wine vinegar
1 teaspoon lemon juice

Salt and freshly ground black
  pepper to taste

4-6 SERVINGS

1. Wash, rinse, and dry well the salad greens. Place them in a salad bowl. Add the sliced onion and toss gently.
2. Preheat the oven to 350° or preheat the broiler. Place 1 slice goat cheese (or crumbled) on the top of each bread slice. Sprinkle the virgin olive oil on the top of the cheese and place a rosemary sprig over all, pressing it down into the cheese. Place the bread slices in an oven-proof dish, and put it either in the oven or under the broiler until the cheese bubbles and begins to melt.
3. Prepare the salad dressing by mixing all the ingredients well. Pour the dressing over the salad, toss it, and then distribute it evenly in six serving plates.
4. Place one cheese—bread slice at the center of each salad plate. Serve immediately.

# Jerusalem Artichoke Salad
## (Salade de Topinambours)

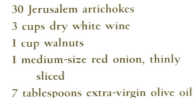

30 Jerusalem artichokes
3 cups dry white wine
1 cup walnuts
1 medium-size red onion, thinly
    sliced
7 tablespoons extra-virgin olive oil

3 tablespoons lemon juice
Salt and freshly ground black
    pepper to taste
1/3 cup finely chopped chervil (or
    parsley), as garnish

6 SERVINGS

1.  Clean the artichokes thoroughly (and as an option, peel them). Place them in a good-size casserole, add the wine, and bring it to a boil. Then lower the heat to medium and cook for about 12–15 minutes. Drain the artichokes and allow them to cool. Cut each in four pieces and place them in a salad bowl. (They can also be cut in slices.)

2.  Place the walnuts in a saucepan, add water, and then boil them for 5 minutes. Drain the walnuts and then crumble with a knife. Add the walnuts and the sliced onion to the artichokes in the bowl.

3.  Prepare a vinaigrette by mixing the olive oil, lemon juice, salt, and pepper thoroughly. Pour over the salad and toss it gently, until the ingredients are evenly coated. Distribute the salad in equal portions onto six serving plates, and sprinkle over each portion some finely chopped chervil (or parsley) as garnish. This is an excellent appetizer any time of the year.

# Grated Carrots and Black Olive Salad

10 large carrots, peeled and sliced
    julienne style
6 branches of parsley, finely
    chopped
3 shallots, thinly sliced

30 medium pitted whole black
    olives
8 tablespoons good olive oil
4 tablespoons wine vinegar
1½ tablespoons Dijon mustard
Salt and freshly ground black
    pepper to taste

6-8 SERVINGS

1. Place the julienned carrots in a big deep bowl. Add the parsley, shallots, and black olives. Mix well.
2. In a separate bowl, place the olive oil, vinegar, mustard, salt, and pepper, and mix thoroughly with a fork until a smooth sauce is achieved.
3. Pour the sauce over the carrot mixture and mix the ingredients well. Refrigerate the salad and keep cold until ready to serve. This is an interesting and easy-to-make appetizer to serve during the warm days of summer.

# Mont St. Michel Shrimp Salad

TEACH YOUR HEART TO GUARD THAT

WHICH YOUR TONGUE TEACHES.

ABBA POEMEN

2 cups shelled cooked shrimp
2 leeks, white parts only, cooked, drained, and sliced
1/2 cup walnut halves
2 apples, peeled, cored, and evenly sliced
2 hard-boiled eggs, coarsely chopped
6 large white mushroom tops, cleaned and thinly sliced

4 tablespoons mayonnaise, homemade or commercial
2 tablespoons olive oil
1 tablespoon lemon juice
1 tablespoon tarragon vinegar (flavored)
1 teaspoon french mustard
Salt to taste
A dash of cayenne pepper
18 lettuce leaves (3 per person)

6 SERVINGS

1. In a large salad bowl arrange and mix well the shrimp, leeks, walnuts, apples, eggs, and mushroom tops. Keep the salad cool until ready to serve.

2. Just before serving, combine in a separate bowl the mayonnaise, oil, lemon juice, vinegar, mustard, salt, and cayenne pepper. Whisk it thoroughly by hand or with a hand mixer. Pour the dressing over the salad and toss it gently.

3. Place 3 lettuce leaves on each plate in a decorative fashion. Arrange the shrimp mixture on the top and serve.

# Asparagus and Artichokes in Tarragon-Scented Vinaigrette

36 fresh spinach leaves (6 per person), trimmed
24 fresh asparagus spears, trimmed
8 tablespoons extra-virgin olive oil
3 tablespoons heavy cream
1 teaspoon french mustard
4 tablespoons tarragon-scented vinegar

Salt and freshly ground black pepper to taste
One 16-ounce jar or can artichoke hearts, drained
2 hard-boiled eggs, finely crumbled
3 teaspoons finely chopped fresh tarragon, as garnish

6 SERVINGS

1. Wash and clean the spinach leaves well. Drain them thoroughly and set them aside.

2. Cook the asparagus in boiling salted water for about 3–4 minutes. Rinse them in cold running water. Drain them thoroughly and dry them with paper towels. Set them aside.

3. Prepare the vinaigrette by combining in a bowl the oil, cream, and mustard. Whisk the mixture with a mixer. Add the vinegar, salt, and pepper, and continue whisking until the vinaigrette achieves a smooth and creamy consistency.

4. Place the spinach leaves in a decorative form on six individual serving plates. Arrange 4 asparagus spears on the top on one side and 2 artichoke hearts on the other side. Pour some of the vinaigrette over them, starting at the center. Garnish the top with some of the crumbled hard-boiled eggs; add some of the finely chopped tarragon on top of the eggs. Serve at room temperature.

# St. Casilda's Spinach Salad

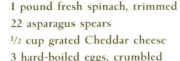

1 pound fresh spinach, trimmed
22 asparagus spears
1/2 cup grated Cheddar cheese
3 hard-boiled eggs, crumbled

4 tablespoons pignoli nuts
1 small red onion, thinly sliced in
   circles

*Dressing*

6 tablespoons extra-virgin olive oil
3 tablespoons lemon juice
2 teaspoons french mustard
4 teaspoons mayonnaise
   (commercial is fine)

1 teaspoon tarragon (fresh or dry),
   chopped if fresh
Salt and freshly ground black
   pepper to taste

6-8 SERVINGS

1. Wash and dry the spinach thoroughly. Place it in a large salad bowl.
2. Boil the asparagus in salted water for 5 minutes. Drain them and slice them 2 inches long. Add them to the spinach. Add the grated cheese, crumbled eggs, pignoli, and onion. Mix the ingredients gently by hand.
3. Just before serving, prepare the dressing by placing all the dressing ingredients in a small bowl and whisking them by hand. Pour the dressing over the salad and toss gently. Serve immediately.

# St. Pelagia Shrimp Salad

1 pound shrimp
1 Vidalia onion, finely chopped
1 cup drained pitted black olives,
    sliced in halves

⅓ cup capers ·
1 medium-size cucumber, thinly
    sliced
1 head leaf lettuce

*Dressing*

6 tablespoons extra-virgin olive oil
3 tablespoons tarragon-scented
    vinegar
1 tablespoon lemon juice

2 teaspoons Dijon mustard
2 tablespoons low-fat plain yogurt
Kosher salt and freshly ground
    black pepper to taste

6 SERVINGS

1. Cook the shrimp in salted water for about 7 minutes. Rinse them under cold water. Shell and devein them. Place them in a deep salad
   bowl.
2. Add the onion, olives, capers, and cucumber to the salad bowl.
3. Wash and dry the lettuce leaves. Place about 3 leaves on each individual plate with the stem part toward the center of the plate.
4. Assemble all the dressing ingredients in a separate bowl and whisk
   them by hand or with a mixer. Pour the dressing over the shrimp mixture and toss the salad gently, making sure all the ingredients are well
   coated. Distribute the shrimp mixture among the plates and serve.

# Potato, Leek, and Egg Salad

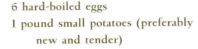

6 hard-boiled eggs
1 pound small potatoes (preferably
   new and tender)

6 leeks

*Vinaigrette*

6 tablespoons extra-virgin olive oil
3 tablespoons tarragon-scented
   vinegar
1/2 teaspoon french mustard

Salt and freshly ground black
   pepper to taste

A bunch of scallions, thinly sliced,
   as garnish

6 SERVINGS

1. Slice the eggs in halves lengthwise.
2. Peel the potatoes and put them in a large casserole filled with water over medium heat. Boil them for about 15 minutes, until they are tender. Drain.
3. Clean and trim the leeks. Discard the green parts. Boil them in salted water for about 15 minutes, until they are cooked. Drain.
4. Prepare the vinaigrette by whisking and mixing well all the ingredients.
5. Place some of the potatoes and 2 egg halves on the center of each plate and gently curb the leeks in a circle around them. Pour some of the vinaigrette evenly over each serving, and top each with some of the thinly sliced scallions as garnish. Serve at room temperature.

SAUCES

# Béchamel Sauce .

3 tablespoons butter (or margarine
   or oil)
2 tablespoons cornstarch
   (or 4 tablespoons flour)
1¹/2 cups milk
Optional: 3 tablespoons dry
   vermouth

Salt and freshly ground black
   pepper to taste
A pinch of nutmeg

ABOUT 2 CUPS

Melt the butter in a good-size stainless steel pan over medium-low heat. Add the cornstarch and stir continuously with a whisk. Add the milk little by little while whisking continuously. Add the vermouth, salt, pepper, and nutmeg and continue stirring. When the sauce begins to boil, reduce the heat to low and continue cooking slowly until it thickens.

NOTE: This sauce is excellent with fish and vegetables, and it is a necessary base for soufflés, omelets, and other egg dishes.

# Mornay Sauce

1½ cups Béchamel Sauce (page 156)
4 tablespoons grated Gruyère
    cheese

4 tablespoons grated Romano
    cheese (or Parmesan cheese)
10 tablespoons heavy cream

2 CUPS

When the Béchamel sauce is at the boiling point, add the cheeses and let them melt as the sauce thickens. Stir continually. When the sauce is ready, remove it from the heat and add the heavy cream while stirring continuously with a whisk or mixer.

# Monastery Mushroom Sauce

A DOG IS BETTER THAN I AM, FOR HE IS

LOVING AND DOES NOT JUDGE

OTHERS.

ABBA XANTHIAS

2 cups mushroom tops, sliced
4 tablespoons butter
4 shallots (or 1 medium-size
    onion), chopped
2 garlic cloves, minced
6 tablespoons dry white wine

1 cup heavy cream
Salt and freshly ground black
    pepper to taste
Finely chopped fresh chervil, as
    needed

6-8 SERVINGS

1. Boil the mushrooms in salted water for about 12–15 minutes. Drain
   and puree the mushrooms in a food processor. Set them aside.
2. Melt the butter over low-medium heat in a nonstick saucepan and add
   the shallots and garlic. Sauté over low heat for 2 or 3 minutes, stirring
   constantly.
3. Add the wine and mix well. Add the cream. Stir and mix well. Add
   the pureed mushrooms, salt, pepper, and some finely chopped chervil.
   Continue stirring until all the ingredients are well blended.

NOTE: This delicious sauce goes well with egg noodles, pasta, rice,
fish, and certain vegetables and egg dishes.

# White Sauce

2 tablespoons cornstarch
 (or 4 tablespoons flour)
1½ cups milk
2 tablespoons butter (or margarine)

Salt and freshly ground black
 pepper to taste
A dash of nutmeg

1½ CUPS

Dissolve the cornstarch in ½ cup of the milk. Melt the butter in a medium-size stainless steel pan over medium heat. When the butter begins foaming, add the milk and cornstarch mixture and stir continuously. Add the remaining 1 cup milk, salt, pepper, and nutmeg and continue to stir until the sauce comes to a boil. Lower the heat and continue stirring until the sauce thickens. The sauce is ready when it is smooth and thick.

NOTE: This sauce can be used as a basis for many other useful variations. It can be used on fish, meats, eggs, and vegetables.

# White Sauce with Mustard

1¹/₂ CUPS

Prepare White Sauce ( page 159 ). Add 2 teaspoons french mustard. Stir until it has been mixed thoroughly.

# White Sauce with Herbs

1¹/₂ CUPS

Prepare White Sauce (page 159). Add 4 tablespoons finely chopped and mixed herbs (tarragon, dill, parsley, thyme, etc.). Also add ¹/₂ teaspoon dry mustard and mix thoroughly.

# White Sauce with Wine

1³/₄ CUPS

Prepare White Sauce (page 159). Add ¼ cup white wine or vermouth and ½ teaspoon dry mustard instead of the nutmeg. Stir thoroughly until well mixed.

# Green Sauce (SAUCE VERTE)

2 CUPS

Prepare White Sauce (page 159). Add ¹/₂ cup white wine and ¹/₂ cup finely chopped parsley. Blend thoroughly during the cooking process. This sauce can be used for a great variety of dishes.

# Green Watercress Sauce

A bunch of watercress, washed and
trimmed
One 10-ounce container plain
yogurt

10 tablespoons heavy cream (or
crème fraîche)
A pinch of nutmeg
Salt and freshly ground black
pepper to taste

ABOUT 1½ CUPS

1. Boil the watercress in salted water no longer than 3 minutes. Rinse it under cold running water. Drain it thoroughly and put it through the food processor.

2. Place the watercress puree in a nonstick saucepan. Add the yogurt, cream, nutmeg, salt, and pepper. Cook over low heat and stir continually until all the ingredients are thoroughly mixed. Keep refrigerated for several hours if you are serving it cold. It can be served hot or cold depending on taste of the chef.

NOTE: It is excellent on fish and certain vegetables when served cold.

# Hollandaise Sauce

½ cup melted butter
3 egg yolks
Juice of ¼ lemon
1 tablespoon salt

¼ teaspoon white pepper
A dash of nutmeg
⅓ cup boiling water

1 CUP

In a bowl, whisk the melted butter with a mixer and add 1 egg yolk at a time while continuing to beat. Add the lemon juice, salt, pepper, and nutmeg and continue whisking with the mixer. Just before serv-ing, place the bowl in a saucepan with boiling water at the bottom. Over low heat, add to the sauce, little by little, the ⅓ cup boiling water while stirring all the time until the sauce thickens. Remove the bowl from the saucepan before serving the sauce. Serve hot.

NOTE: This sauce can be used on fish, veal, egg, and vegetable dishes.

# Monastery Tomato Sauce

6 tablespoons olive oil
1 large onion, finely chopped
3 garlic cloves, minced
2 pounds fresh tomatoes, peeled
    and sliced
3 tablespoons tomato puree
1 carrot, peeled and finely chopped

4 tablespoons finely chopped fresh
    basil
1 bay leaf
Salt and freshly ground black
    pepper to taste
A pinch of thyme

2 CUPS

Heat the olive oil to low-medium in an enamel or stainless steel saucepan and slowly sauté the onion and garlic for a few minutes until they are soft and transparent. Add the rest of the ingredients. Lower the heat to low and cook slowly for about 30—40 minutes, stirring from time to time. While the sauce is cooking, cover the saucepan partially, so that the sauce remains moist and juicy. When the sauce is done, turn off the heat, cover the pan, and let it sit for a few minutes before serving. (Remove the bay leaf.)

# Sauce Provençal

6 tablespoons extra-virgin olive oil
1 pound ripe tomatoes, peeled,
    seeded, and sliced in quarters
1 large onion, coarsely chopped
1 medium-size carrot, peeled and
    thinly sliced
3 garlic cloves, peeled and minced

One 10-ounce can pitted black
    olives, drained
1 bay leaf
A pinch of thyme (fresh or dried)
Salt and freshly ground black
    pepper to taste

ABOUT 2 CUPS

1. Pour the oil into a nonstick casserole and heat it over medium heat. When the oil is hot add the tomatoes, onion, carrot, garlic, olives, bay leaf, thyme, salt, and pepper. Cook for about 5 minutes, then lower the heat to low-medium. Stir well.

2. Cover the casserole, and gently simmer the sauce. Stir from time to time. If the heat seems high, reduce it to low. Cook for about 25–30 minutes. Check the seasonings and serve.

NOTE: This sauce is excellent with pasta, polenta, rice, certain fish, and vegetables.

# Pesto Sauce (Sauce au Pistou)

6 garlic cloves, minced
1/2 cup basil leaves, finely chopped
1/2 cup well-chopped pistachio nuts

1 cup olive oil, or more
8 teaspoons grated Parmesan cheese
A pinch of salt

1 CUP

Place the garlic and basil in a mortar and mash with a pestle. Add the pistachio nuts and continue mashing the ingredients thoroughly. Place the mixture in a larger container, add the olive oil gradually, then the cheese and salt, and blend thoroughly.

NOTES: A simpler and quicker way to prepare the pesto sauce is to place all the ingredients in a blender and mix thoroughly.

This sauce is usually used with pasta, but it can also be used with gnocchi, seafood, eggs, and vegetables like zucchini.

# Red Wine Sauce

3 shallots, finely chopped
5 tablespoons water
2 cups good red wine (Bordeaux or other)
1 bay leaf

4 tablespoons butter
A pinch of cayenne pepper
Salt and freshly ground black pepper to taste
1 teaspoon cornstarch

2 CUPS

1. Place the shallots and 4 tablespoons of the water in a nonstick casserole. Cook over medium heat for about 2 minutes. Add the wine and bay leaf. Bring to a quick boil, then reduce the heat to low-medium and cook for about 8–10 minutes.

2. Add the butter and mix well. Add the cayenne pepper, salt, and pepper, and mix some more. Dilute the cornstarch in the remaining 1 tablespoon water and add to the wine sauce. Continue stirring for about 1–2 minutes until the sauce is formed. Remove the bay leaf before serving.

NOTE: This sauce is excellent over certain meat dishes, as well as over beans, especially red beans.

# Roquefort Sauce

2 ounces Roquefort cheese,
    crumbled
4 tablespoons heavy cream
2 tablespoons (¼ stick) butter
½ cup dry white wine
1 tablespoon cornstarch

½ cup vegetable broth (or chicken
    broth)
Freshly ground black pepper to
    taste
Salt to taste, if needed

1½ CUPS

1. Place the cheese, cream, butter, and wine in a nonstick saucepan. Heat over medium heat, stirring constantly, until a sauce is formed.

2. Dilute the cornstarch in the broth and add to the sauce. Add the pepper (salt only if needed). Continue stirring for several minutes until a thicker sauce consistency is achieved. Serve hot.

NOTE: This is an excellent sauce for vegetables like asparagus, broccoli, and cauliflower.

# Onion Sauce (Sauce aux Oignons)

2 ounces (¹/₂ stick) butter
4 medium-size onions, finely
   chopped
1 cup dry white wine

Salt and freshly ground black
   pepper to taste
¹/₂ cup heavy cream

2 CUPS

Melt the butter over low-medium heat in a saucepan. Add the onions and sauté them over medium heat for a few minutes. Add the wine, salt, and pepper and cook slowly over low heat about 15–20 minutes, stirring from time to time. At the end, add the heavy cream and mix thoroughly. Serve hot.

NOTE: This sauce can be used on eggs, potatoes, seafood, and certain meats.

# Thick Asparagus Sauce

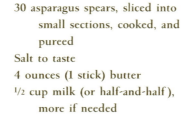

30 asparagus spears, sliced into small sections, cooked, and pureed
Salt to taste
4 ounces (1 stick) butter
1/2 cup milk (or half-and-half), more if needed

Finely grated zest of 1 lemon
Freshly ground black pepper to taste
A pinch of sugar
Optional: 3 tablespoons dry white wine

6-8 SERVINGS

Melt the butter in a saucepan over low-medium heat. Add the milk (or half-and-half), grated lemon zest, pepper, sugar, and wine (if used). Whisk continually for about 4–5 minutes. Add the asparagus puree and continue whisking until the ingredients are well blended. Check the seasonings and serve hot. Otherwise, place it in the refrigerator and reheat it just before serving.

NOTE: This sauce can be used in many varied ways: over omelets and fish, over vegetables like potatoes and turnips.

# Parsley Sauce (Sauce au Persil)

½ cup white wine
6 shallots, sliced and minced
1 bay leaf
1 cup vegetable stock

1½ cups heavy cream
Salt and freshly ground black
    pepper to taste
1 cup finely chopped fresh parsley

2 CUPS

Pour the wine into a good-size saucepan, add the shallots and the bay leaf. Bring the wine to a boil while stirring constantly. Add the stock and continue stirring until it comes to a boil again. Lower the heat to low-medium and continue boiling for 3 or 4 minutes, until the sauce is reduced to about ¾ cup. At this point, add the cream, salt, and pepper. Blend and bring the sauce to another boil. Add the parsley and continue cooking and stirring for another 5–6 minutes. Blend the sauce well, remove from the heat, and allow it to cool. Remove the bay leaf. When cool, pass the sauce through the blender. Pour the sauce back into the saucepan, and reheat it for 1–2 minutes, stirring all the while. Serve hot.

NOTE: This sauce can be used in a variety of ways, either over fish, vegetables, or egg dishes.

# Benedictine Chutney Sauce

4 tablespoons olive oil
1/2 pound ripe tomatoes, peeled,
    seeded, and coarsely chopped
1 large onion, chopped
3 garlic cloves, peeled and minced
1/2 pound apples, peeled, cored, and
    sliced
1 medium-size zucchini, cubed
1 1/2 cups cider vinegar

One 1.5-ounce package raisins
Sugar (brown or granulated) to
    taste
Salt and freshly ground black
    pepper to taste
1 teaspoon cumin
A pinch of nutmeg
1 teaspoon coriander seeds

ABOUT 1 1/2 CUPS

1. Pour the oil into a large nonstick casserole and add the rest of the ingredients. Simmer over low heat, stirring often, until the mixture becomes saucy and thick, about 25–30 minutes. Check the seasonings and when the chutney is done, turn off the heat and allow it to cool.

2. If the chutney is not going to be served immediately but in the next few days, pour it into a bowl and keep it, tightly covered, in the refrigerator. Otherwise, sterilize some canning jars, pour the chutney into them, cover the jars, and place them in a bath of boiling water for 20 minutes, until the jars are thoroughly sealed.

NOTE: It accompanies lentil and rice dishes well, as well as certain meats.

# Sauce Delight (WITH GORGONZOLA CHEESE)

1 cup milk
1 tablespoon cornstarch
2 tablespoons olive oil (or 1
    tablespoon butter)
1/4 cup dry white vermouth

4 tablespoons grated Gorgonzola
    cheese
A pinch of nutmeg
Salt and freshly ground black
    pepper to taste

FOR 4-6 SERVINGS

1. Pour the milk into a small bowl. Add the cornstarch and stir until the cornstarch is totally diluted in the milk.
2. Pour the olive oil into a medium-size saucepan, add the milk mixture, and stir continually over medium heat until the mixture slowly begins to thicken.
3. Whisk in gradually the vermouth, then the cheese, and reduce the heat to low or low-medium. Add the nutmeg, salt, and pepper, and continue stirring until the sauce reaches a thick rich consistency. Keep the sauce warm until ready to serve.

NOTE: This is an excellent sauce to serve over noodles, pasta, potatoes, broccoli, cauliflower, brussels sprouts, etc.

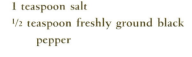

# Simple Vinaigrette (Vinaigrette Classique)

1 teaspoon salt
1/2 teaspoon freshly ground black
  pepper

3 tablespoons wine vinegar
6 tablespoons extra-virgin olive oil

ABOUT 1/2 CUP

Place the salt and pepper in a cup or bowl. Add the vinegar and stir thoroughly. Add the oil and stir until all the ingredients are completely blended.

HOW FREE YOU CAN BECOME IF YOU STOP WORRYING ABOUT THINGS THAT DON'T CONCERN YOU! THE FIRST THING FOR A CONTEMPLATIVE IS TO MIND HIS OWN BUSINESS, AND ALL CARE OF YOURSELF, PHYSICALLY, MATERIALLY, IS NO LONGER YOUR BUSINESS. IT IS IN THE HANDS OF SOMEBODY ELSE—GOD.

THOMAS MERTON

# Vinaigrette with Mustard

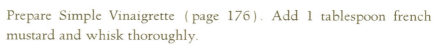

(Vinaigrette à la Moutarde)

ABOUT ½ CUP

Prepare Simple Vinaigrette (page 176). Add 1 tablespoon french mustard and whisk thoroughly.

# Vinaigrette with Garlic (Vinaigrette à l'Ail)

ABOUT ½ CUP

Prepare Simple Vinaigrette (page 176). Add 1 crushed garlic clove, well minced. Let the vinaigrette stand for a few hours before using.

—BUT BEAUTY ABSOLUTE, SEPARATE,

SIMPLE AND EVERLASTING.

PLATO

# Vinaigrette with Herbs
(VINAIGRETTE AUX HERBES)

ABOUT ½ CUP

Prepare Simple Vinaigrette ( page 176 ). but replace the vinegar with the equivalent of lemon juice. Add ¼ cup finely chopped herbs ( parsley, tarragon, chervil, etc. ). Mix thoroughly.

# Sauce Mayonnaise

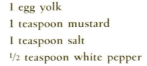

1 egg yolk
1 teaspoon mustard
1 teaspoon salt
1/2 teaspoon white pepper

About 3/4 cup light olive oil
(or vegetable oil)
2 teaspoons lemon juice
(or tarragon vinegar)

I CUP

Place the egg yolk in a bowl, add the mustard, salt, and pepper and begin to mix with a whisk or a mixer. (It is simpler with a mixer.) Add the oil little by little while continuing to mix. In between add the lemon juice and then resume adding the oil until the mayonnaise thickens properly. Keep the mayonnaise in the refrigerator until it is ready to be used.

NOTE: The mayonnaise can be used in many ways: with hard-boiled eggs, potato salad, Russian potato salad, asparagus.

# Light Mayonnaise

1 egg yolk
One 8-ounce container plain yogurt
½ teaspoon french mustard
2 tablespoons lemon juice

2 tablespoons olive oil
Salt and freshly ground black
    pepper to taste

6 SERVINGS

Place all the above ingredients in a deep bowl. With the help of a mixer whisk all the ingredients thoroughly until the mayonnaise reaches a thick consistency. Refrigerate until ready to be used. This mayonnaise can be used over fish, hard-boiled eggs, on potato salad, etc. And it can easily replace the regular, richer mayonnaise, in a recipe. Will keep for one week if refrigerated.

NOTE: When this sauce is used over fish or beets, add 1 teaspoon finely chopped fresh dill.

# Garlic Sauce (Sauce Aioli)

1 CUP

Prepare Sauce Mayonnaise (page 180). Add 5 minced garlic cloves. Mix thoroughly and place the sauce in the refrigerator for several hours before using it.

NOTE: This sauce can be used on seafood, salads, vegetables, and meats served cold.

HOW SIMPLE WE MUST GROW, HOW

SIMPLE THEY WHO CAME!

THE SHEPHERDS LOOKED AT GOD

BEFORE ALL OTHER MEN.

HE SEES GOD NEVERMORE, NOT THERE,

NOT HERE ON EARTH

WHO DOES NOT LONG WITHIN TO BE

A SHEPHERD FIRST.

ANGELUS SILESIUS

# Tarragon Sauce "Classique"

( Sauce à l'Estragon )

¹/₂ cup sour cream
3 tablespoons lemon juice
¹/₂ cup heavy cream

3 tablespoons chopped fresh
    tarragon
Salt and freshly ground black
    pepper to taste

1 CUP

Place all the ingredients in a deep bowl and use a mixer to stir and blend thoroughly. Refrigerate until it is time to use. It can be used on salads and seafoods.

# Crème Fraîche

1 cup heavy cream (not ultrapasteurized)

1 cup dairy sour cream

2 CUPS

Whisk the heavy cream and sour cream together in a bowl. Cover loosely with plastic wrap and let sit in kitchen or other warm place overnight, or until thickened. Refrigerate for at least 4 hours. The crème fraîche will then be thick and ready to use. It will last for up to 2 weeks in the refrigerator.

SIMPLICITY MEANS THIS: TO KNOW

NOTHING OF GUILE

AND ON GOOD WORKS ALONE TO

HUMBLY SET ONE'S EYE.

ANGELUS SILESIUS

# Cold Spicy Sauce Napoleon

2 tablespoons lemon juice
One 10-ounce container plain
    yogurt (or low-fat sour cream)
1/2 teaspoon french mustard
1/2 teaspoon curry powder
1/2 teaspoon paprika

1/2 teaspoon cumin
1/2 teaspoon coriander grains
1 garlic clove, finely minced
A pinch of salt
A pinch of cayenne pepper

6 SERVINGS

Place all the ingredients in a deep bowl and mix well with a mixer or
with a fork. Keep the sauce in the refrigerator until it is ready to be
used.

NOTE: This is an excellent sauce to be served over cold vegetables
such as asparagus or potatoes, or over cold salmon.

# Cold Tarragon Sauce

One 8-ounce container sour cream
1 egg yolk
2 tablespoons lemon juice
1 tablespoon french mustard

2 teaspoons finely chopped tarragon
(fresh or dried)
Salt and freshly ground pepper to
taste

6 SERVINGS

Place all the ingredients in a deep bowl and whisk with a mixer until the sauce reaches a thick consistency. Check the seasonings. Keep the sauce in the refrigerator until it is ready to be used.

NOTE: It is an excellent sauce over hard-boiled eggs, cold meats or fish, and certain vegetables such as asparagus, etc.

12

BREADS

# Monastery Brioche

One 1/4-ounce package active dry
  yeast
1/4 cup warm water
4 cups all-purpose flour
1/2 teaspoon salt
1/4 cup milk

2 tablespoons sugar
2 tablespoons honey
6 eggs, beaten
6 ounces butter, plus about 2
  tablespoons

1 BIG LOAF

1. Dissolve the yeast in the warm water. Pour the yeast-water mixture into a deep bowl and add 1 cup of flour. Grease your hands with a bit of lard or butter, and then mix the ingredients well and shape them into a ball. Cover the bowl with a wet towel and place it in a warm place for about 45 minutes.

2. Put the rest of the flour into a large mixing bowl. Make a hollow space in the center of the flour and add there the salt, milk, sugar, honey, eggs, and 3 ounces of the butter, cut into small pieces. Work the mixture with your greasy fingers, gradually mixing the flour with the other ingredients. When a dough is formed, place it on a floured board and work it with your hands until the dough turns mellow and smooth. Punch it a couple of times with your fist.

3. Cut another 3 ounces of the butter into small pieces and gradually add it to the dough, without necessarily working the dough—simply mix and blend the butter into it. At this point add the rising ball (yeast-flour mixture) and gently work and blend it with the dough.

4. Again, shape the dough into a ball and place it in a clean bowl. Cover the bowl with a wet towel and this time let it stand at room temperature for several hours until the dough has doubled in size. Punch down the dough and put it in the refrigerator for at least 4 hours or overnight.

5. Remove the dough from the refrigerator, punch down the dough, and shape it into the form of the mold to be used for baking, either a brioche mold, or bread pan, or other. Butter thoroughly the mold, and place the dough into it, filling two thirds of the mold. Cover with a wet towel and let the dough stand for 45 minutes or so, until it rises and again doubles in size.

6. Preheat the oven to 400°. Melt the remaining butter—about 2 tablespoons—and then brush it on the top of the dough. With a small sharp knife gently make a cross at the center of the dough. Place the mold in the oven for about 25–30 minutes, until the brioche has browned on the top or a thin knife inserted into the brioche comes out clean. When the brioche is done, remove it from the oven, and allow it to cool on a rack before serving.

# St. Maur Onion Bread

1 good-size onion, finely chopped
1/3 cup olive oil
1/2 cup milk
4 tablespoons honey
2 teaspoons salt

1 cup water
One 1/4-ounce package active dry
 yeast
3 cups whole wheat flour
2 cups white flour

*Optional*

1/2 cup grated Cheddar cheese, as
 needed

1/3 cup finely chopped onion

2 LOAVES

1. In a non-stick saucepan over low-medium heat sauté the onion briefly in the olive oil until the onion begins to turn golden. Add the milk, honey, and salt and stir until the ingredients are well blended. Keep it simmering over low heat.

2. In a separate saucepan heat the water to lukewarm. Stir in the yeast. Remove from the heat and let stand for about 5 minutes.

3. Pour the water-yeast mixture into a good-size bowl. Add the onion-milk mixture and stir gently. Gradually add both flours. Grease your hands and begin to form a dough. Knead the dough on a surface covered with flour for about 3 minutes.

4. Grease well another large bowl or saucepan. Place the dough into it. Cover it with a wet or damp kitchen towel. Put it in a dark, warm place until the dough doubles in size (approximately 1–1 1/2 hours).

5. Punch down the dough and divide it in two halves. Knead again for about 1 or 2 minutes and form 2 separate loaves. Place the loaves on greased bread pans. Cover them with the damp towel and let them rise again until they double in size (approximately the same time).

6. Preheat the oven to 350°. Place the bread pans in the oven and bake for about 30–35 minutes, until the tops turn brown and crispy.

7. If desired, before the last 5 minutes of baking, spread the grated cheese on the top of the loaves and sprinkle the chopped onion on top of the cheese.

# St. Placid Whole Wheat Bread

SIMPLICITY, LETTING GO OF OPINIONS
AND CRAVING, IS AN ACT OF
COMPASSION FOR OURSELVES. WHEN
WE LET GO OF YEARNING FOR THE
FUTURE, PREOCCUPATION WITH THE
PAST, AND STRATEGIES TO PROTECT
THE PRESENT, THERE IS NOWHERE LEFT
TO GO BUT WHERE WE ARE. TO
CONNECT WITH THE PRESENT MOMENT
IS TO BEGIN TO APPRECIATE THE
BEAUTY OF TRUE SIMPLICITY.

JACK KORNFIELD AND
CHRISTINA FELDMAN

3 cups whole wheat flour (stone-
     ground if possible)
2½ teaspoons salt
Two ¼-ounce packages active dry
     yeast
2½ cups milk

¼ cup molasses (or honey)
¼ cup vegetable oil
1 egg, well beaten
½ cup all-purpose white flour
½ cup wheat germ

2 LOAVES

1. Combine 2 cups of the whole wheat flour with the salt and 1 yeast package in a good-size mixing bowl.

2. Heat the milk over low heat to the point between lukewarm and warm. Add the molasses and vegetable oil. Stir until both are well blended with the milk. Remove from the heat and stir in the second yeast package. Let it stand for 5 minutes.

3. Gradually add the milk mixture to the flour. Then add the beaten egg. Gradually add the remaining flour, both whole wheat and white, and the wheat germ. With greased hands, work to form a dough. Sprinkle flour over a flat surface, and gently knead the dough for about 2 minutes, until it becomes soft and smooth.

4. Grease well another large bowl or casserole and place the dough into it. Cover it with a damp cloth or towel. Put it in a dark, warm place and let the dough rise until it doubles in size (approximately 1 hour).

5. Punch down the dough and divide it in two equal halves. Knead again for 1 minute, form each half into a loaf, and then place the loaves on well-greased bread pans. Cover them with a damp cloth or towel and let them rise again until double in size.

6. Preheat the oven to 350°. Place the bread pans in the oven and bake for about 40–45 minutes until the loaves turn golden on the top and sound hollow when tapped.

Remove the bread from the pans immediately and allow them to cool on racks.

# St. Anthony's Bread

One 1/4-ounce package active dry
yeast
3 teaspoons sesame seeds
1/2 plus 1/3 cups water
2 cups whole wheat flour

3 tablespoons finely chopped fresh
chives
1 tablespoon salt
Cornmeal, as needed

2 LOAVES

1. Place the yeast and sesame seeds in a good-size bowl. Gradually stir in 1/2 cup water until the yeast is dissolved. Gradually add the remaining 1/3 cup water.
2. Gradually add the flour, chives, and salt. Stir continually until a dough is formed.
3. Place the dough on a surface covered with flour, and knead gently for about 12 minutes. Place the dough in a large, oiled bowl or casserole. Cover it with a damp towel and allow the dough to rise in a warm place for about 1 hour, until it doubles in size.
4. After the dough rises, punch it down, and knead once again for about 6–8 minutes. Sprinkle two large baking sheets with cornmeal. Divide the dough in two equal parts and shape them into balls. Flatten them a bit at the center, and place them on the baking sheets.
5. Cover the balls with towels and again let them rise until double in size, approximately 30–45 minutes.
6. Preheat the oven to 400°. Place the sheets in the oven. Bake the loaves for about 40–45 minutes, until they turn brown and crispy on top. Allow the bread to cool on racks before serving.

# Avignon Banana and Raisin Bread

2 eggs
6 tablespoons honey (or maple
    syrup)
1 tablespoon vanilla extract
4 medium-size bananas

1¼ cups whole wheat flour
2 teaspoons baking powder
One 1.5-ounce package dried raisins
5 tablespoons butter (or margarine)

I LOAF

1. In a large mixing bowl beat the eggs lightly. Add the honey and vanilla, and mix well.
2. Mash the bananas thoroughly and add them to the egg mixture. Mix them well.
3. In a separate bowl mix the flour and baking powder and stir gently, little by little, into the banana-egg mixture. Add the raisins and continue mixing.
4. Melt the butter and stir it into the mixture until the ingredients are evenly blended. Do not overwork the mixture.
5. Preheat the oven to 350°. Butter thoroughly a bread pan and pour the banana batter into it. Bake for about 45–50 minutes. Insert a clean thin knife in the center of the loaf to check if the bread is done (the knife will come out clean). Remove it from the oven, allow it to cool a bit before unmolding. Slice and serve.

# Laudate Oatmeal Bread

SEEK GOD IN THE SIMPLICITY OF YOUR

HEART.

SAINT BERNARD

2 cups water
3/4 cup margarine
Two 1.5-ounce packages raisins
2 cups oatmeal
2/3 cup brown sugar (or granulated
  sugar)

2 cups whole wheat flour
2 teaspoons baking powder
1 teaspoon baking soda
2 large eggs, beaten

2 LOAVES

1. Preheat the oven to 350°.

2. Bring the water to a boil and add the margarine. Stir until the margarine dissolves in the water. Turn off the heat. Add the raisins, oatmeal, and sugar. Stir well and allow the mixture to stand until the oatmeal absorbs all the water.

3. In a deep bowl blend well the flour, baking powder, and baking soda. Add the beaten eggs to the flour, and work with a fork to combine and mix the ingredients well.

4. Add the oatmeal mixture to the flour mixture and with lightly wet hands work on the dough until it becomes even and uniform. Divide the mixture into two even portions.

5. Grease thoroughly two bread pans and place the dough into them. Bake for 30–40 minutes until the top starts turning deep brown. Insert a thin knife in the center; if it comes out clean, the bread is done. Allow it to cool before serving.

## 13

FRUITS AND DESSERTS

# Monaco Cherry Bread Pudding

6 cups cubed whole wheat country
    bread
One 16-ounce can pitted black
    cherries, drained
2 medium-size pears, peeled and
    cut into small pieces
2 medium-size apples, peeled and
    cut into small pieces

1 cup blanched almonds
1 cup sweet sherry
4 cups milk
1/2 cup sugar
2 teaspoons Calvados liqueur
5 eggs, separated

8 SERVINGS

1. Preheat the oven to 300°. Put the bread cubes on an ovenproof tray. Place it in the oven for about 12 minutes, until the bread is lightly toasted.

2. Place the cherries, pears, apples, and almonds in a casserole. Add the sherry and simmer gently over low heat for about 10 minutes until most of the liquid evaporates. Stir from time to time. Cover the casserole and let it stand.

3. In a very large bowl whisk the milk, sugar, Calvados, and egg yolks. Gradually add the bread cubes and the fruit mixture. Mix all the ingredients well.

4. Beat the egg whites until stiff and add about half of it to the bread-fruit mixture. Mix gently.

5. Pour the mixture into a long, rectangular, buttered baking dish. Spread evenly and spread the remaining egg whites over the top. Bake for about 40–45 minutes. Allow it to cool a bit before serving.

# Henry IV Fig Compote

3 cups sweet wine
3/4 cup brown sugar (or granulated sugar)
1 pound dried figs, stemmed

1/2 cup dark raisins
5 cloves
1 tablespoon lemon juice

6 SERVINGS

1. Pour the wine into a saucepan. Add the sugar and bring it to a quick boil. Add the figs, raisins, cloves, and lemon juice and lower the heat to low-medium.

2. Cook the figs for about 15 minutes, stirring from time to time. Remove the figs and raisins and place them in a serving bowl, or on six individual dessert plates.

3. Continue cooking the liquid (the wine) until it slowly turns into syrup. Turn off the heat, remove the cloves, allow the syrup to cool, and then pour it over the figs before serving them. Serve the compote lukewarm.

# Acorn Squash Soufflé

THE MONK IS A MAN OF ONE-NESS,

SIMPLICITY: HIS VERY NAME SAYS IT,

MONACHOS: ALONE, SINGLE, SIMPLE.

ESTHER DE WAAL

2 medium-size acorn squash
1/2 teaspoon salt, plus a dash
4 tablespoons (1/2 stick) sweet
   butter
1/4 cup cornstarch
1 1/2 cups milk

1/4 cup pure maple syrup
1/2 teaspoon cinnamon
A dash of nutmeg
2 teaspoons vanilla extract
5 eggs, separated
1/3 cup sugar

6 SERVINGS

1. Slice the squash in half; scoop out the seeds, and clean the insides well. Place the squash upside down in a large pot filled with water. Add the dash of salt and bring the water to a boil. Cook the squash for about 20 minutes. Drain and allow them to cool.

2. With the help of a pointed spoon scoop the squash pulp into a bowl. Mash the squash thoroughly.

3. Melt the butter in a casserole over low-medium heat. Dissolve the cornstarch in the milk and add gradually to the melted butter while stirring continually. Add the maple syrup, the remaining 1/2 teaspoon salt, cinnamon, nutmeg, and vanilla. Continue to stir until the mixture begins to thicken and all the ingredients are well blended. Remove the casserole from the heat.

4. Preheat the oven to 350°. In a large bowl beat the egg yolks with a mixer. Gradually add the squash, the cornstarch mixture, and the sugar. Continue beating with the mixer until the mixture becomes smooth and well blended.

5. In a separate bowl beat the egg whites stiff with a clean mixer. Add about 1/2 cup of the stiffened egg whites to the squash mixture and fold it in. Pour this mixture into a well-buttered good-size soufflé

dish. Then, with the help of a spatula, fold the remaining stiffened egg whites into the mixture. Bake for about 45 minutes. Serve the soufflé hot.

NOTE: This is a lovely dessert to serve throughout the cold winter months and on special occasions like Thanksgiving and other winter festal days.

# St. Peter's Zabaglione

1 pint raspberries
1 pint strawberries
6 egg yolks
3/4 cup granulated sugar

3/4 cup sweet vermouth (good quality)
3/4 cup heavy cream
4 tablespoons confectioners' sugar
A dash of vanilla extract

6 SERVINGS

1. Wash and drain the fruit. Set it aside.
2. Place the egg yolks in a deep metal bowl. Add the sugar and vermouth.
3. Place the metal bowl over a pot containing slow-simmering water and whip the egg mixture with a mixer until it reaches a thick consistency. Refrigerate for about 2 hours.
4. Into a separate bowl, pour the heavy cream, confectioners' sugar, and vanilla extract. Whip until stiff. Mix half of this with the egg yolk mixture, and set the other half aside to be used as garnish.
5. Divide the fruit among six glass bowls or serving dishes. Pour the sauce evenly over the fruit. Top each serving with some of the remaining whipped cream. Serve cold.

# Country-Style Compote

1 butternut squash, peeled, seeded, and cubed

About 4 cups water

4 apples, peeled, cored, and sliced in quarters

½ pound dried prunes, pitted and cut in halves

A bunch of cloves

½ cup sugar

1 lemon rind, grated

1 teaspoon cinnamon

3 tablespoons Calvados liqueur (or other apple or pear liqueur)

6-8 SERVINGS

1. Place the squash cubes in a large saucepan, add the water, and bring to a boil. Reduce the heat to medium, cover the saucepan, and cook for 15 minutes more or less, until the squash is tender.

2. Add the apples, prunes, cloves, sugar, lemon rind, cinnamon, and liqueur. Cover the saucepan and continue cooking for another 15 minutes. Stir occasionally.

3. When the compote is done, remove the lemon rind and check the seasonings. Allow the compote to cool and then place it in the refrigerator for several hours before serving. Serve cold.

# Empress Eugénie Rice Pudding

## ( Riz à l'Impératrice Eugénie )

$^{2}/_{3}$ cup white rice

4 cups water

6 cups milk

1 vanilla bean, cut into 2 pieces

1 cup granulated sugar

$^{1}/_{2}$ cup raisins

6 egg yolks

A pinch of cinnamon, plus more, as garnish

Finely grated rind of 1 lemon

1 cup heavy cream

$^{1}/_{3}$ cup confectioners' sugar

4-6 SERVINGS

1. Place the rice in a saucepan, add the water, bring to a boil, and cook for 5 minutes. Drain.

2. Pour 3 cups of the milk into a nonstick saucepan, add the rice, half the vanilla bean, and $^{1}/_{2}$ cup of the granulated sugar. Cook over low-medium heat until the rice is cooked and has thickened (about 20–30 minutes). Toward the end of the cooking add the raisins and mix well.

3. Beat the egg yolks with the remaining $^{1}/_{2}$ cup granulated sugar in the top of a double boiler over low-medium heat. Mix well until the mixture becomes smooth and creamy. Heat the remaining 3 cups milk in a separate pan, and when hot, pour it gradually into the egg mixture. Add also the other half of the vanilla bean. Continue cooking over low-medium heat until the custard thickens. Stir continually. At the end of the cooking, add the pinch of cinnamon and grated lemon. Mix well and remove the vanilla beans. Turn off the heat and allow the custard to cool.

4. In a deep bowl whip the cream and the confectioners' sugar with the help of a mixer until the mixture becomes a Chantilly (whipped cream). Fold the Chantilly into the rice gradually, then add the custard and blend well. Chill for several hours before serving. Just before serving, sprinkle some cinnamon on the top of the rice pudding.

# Anjou Baked Pears

4 Anjou pears, peeled and sliced in
    perfect halves
8 teaspoons maple syrup
brown sugar (or granulated sugar),
    as needed

4 tablespoons (1/2 stick) butter
1/2 cup heavy cream
4 egg whites, beaten stiff

4 SERVINGS

1. Preheat the oven to 350°. Butter thoroughly an elongated ovenproof dish.
2. Carefully scoop out with a pear knife the seeds at the core of the fruit. Arrange the pears on the baking dish closely packed next to one another.
3. Pour 1 teaspoon maple syrup on the top of each pear half at the center and let it run over. Sprinkle brown sugar over the surface of the pears. Cut the butter into small bits and distribute it over the pears. Place the dish in the oven and bake for about 20 minutes.
4. Pour the heavy cream evenly over all the pears and with a spatula spoon the egg whites over the top. Place the dish back in the oven for another 10 minutes or so, until the egg whites turn brown. Serve warm.

# Lemon Tart à la Provençale
## (Tarte au Citron à la Provençale)

YOU CAN TELL HOW A MONK PRAYS BY

THE WAY IN WHICH HE SWEEPS THE

CLOISTER.

AN OLD MONASTIC SAYING

*Pastry*

1 egg
1 cup flour
4 ounces (1 stick) sweet butter

4 tablespoons ice water
A pinch of salt

*Filling*

1/2 cup fresh lemon juice
1/2 cup sugar
1 tablespoon vanilla extract
1/3 cup almonds, finely grond

4 tablespoons crème fraîche (or
    sour cream)
4 eggs

6 SERVINGS

1. Prepare the pastry shell by mixing all the ingredients in a good-size bowl. Use both a fork and your hands for mixing. Do not overwork the dough. Form a ball and sprinkle it with flour. Place the dough in the refrigerator for at least 1 hour and let it rest.

2. Preheat the oven to 300°. When the dough is ready to be worked, sprinkle some flour over a board or working kitchen table and carefully roll out the dough, extending it in every direction. Butter thoroughly a tart or pie dish and carefully place the rolled-out dough in it. Trim the edges in a decorative fashion. Cover the pastry with foil and place it in the oven for about 15 minutes to prebake the crust. (Pierce the dough all over with a fork, before placing it in the oven.) And pierce it again during the prebaking period if the crust begins to bubble. Remove the pastry crust from the oven and allow it to cool for 12–15 minutes. Don't turn off the oven.

3.  Whisk the lemon juice, sugar, vanilla, and almonds in a bowl until the mixture is thoroughly blended. Add the crème fraîche and whisk some more. Whisk the eggs in a separate bowl with a mixer, and then whisk them into the lemon mixture in small amounts at a time. The mixture must be smooth and evenly blended.

4.  Pour the lemon mixture into the crust and bake for about 30 minutes. Allow the tart to cool for at least 1 hour, then cut it into six slices and serve. During the summer months, the tart may be refrigerated for several hours and afterward served cold.

# St. Simeon Orange Tart

## (TARTE À L'ORANGE)

*Pastry*

1 egg
1 cup flour
4 ounces (1 stick) butter (or
    margarine)

1/4 cup sugar
A pinch of salt
6 tablespoons ice water

*Filling*

4 eggs
3/4 cup sugar
1 1/4 cups freshly squeezed orange
    juice

Grated zest of 4 oranges
1 tablespoon orange liqueur (or
    other similar liqueur)
4 ounces (1 stick) butter

6 SERVINGS

1. Prepare the pastry shell by mixing all the ingredients in a large, deep bowl. (This can also be done in a food processor.) Use both a fork and your hands for mixing. Do not overwork the dough. Form a ball with the dough and sprinkle with flour. Place the dough in the refrigerator for at least 1 hour and let it rest.

2. Preheat the oven to 250°–300°. When the dough is ready to be worked, sprinkle some flour over the table or a board and carefully roll out the dough, extending it in every direction.

3. Butter a deep tart pan or pie dish, and place the rolled dough in it. Adjust the dough to the dish and trim the edges in a decorative fashion. Cover the pastry shell with aluminum foil and place it in the oven for about 10–12 minutes to prebake. Then remove it and set aside. Raise the oven temperature to 375°.

4. To prepare the filling, beat the eggs in a deep bowl. Gradually add the sugar, while continue to beat with a mixer. Gradually add the orange juice, and continue mixing. Add the grated orange zest and orange liqueur and mix well.

5. Melt the butter and then gradually add and stir it into the orange mixture. Blend well and pour the mixture into the pastry shell. Fill about two-thirds of the tart dish. Bake for about 30 minutes, until the mixture becomes firm and the shell turns brown. Allow it to cool before serving. It may also be refrigerated and served cold during the summer months.

# Dauphin Easy Apple Soufflé

4 Golden Delicious apples, peeled, cored, and sliced
1/2 cup sugar, plus 4 tablespoons
1/2 teaspoon cinnamon
3 eggs, separated

1 1/2 cups milk
1/2 cup white all-purpose flour
1/2 teaspoon baking powder
3 tablespoons Calvados liqueur

4-6 SERVINGS

1. Preheat the oven to 350°. Butter thoroughly a long baking dish. Arrange the apple slices evenly over the surface of the dish. Sprinkle 4 tablespoons of the sugar and the cinnamon over the apples.
2. Place the egg yolks in a blender, add the milk, and whirl thoroughly. Add the remaining 1/2 cup sugar and the rest of the ingredients, except the egg whites, and whirl some more until well blended.
3. Beat the egg whites stiff with a mixer and fold them into the egg yolk mixture with a spatula. Spread it over the entire top of the apples. Place the dish in the oven and bake for about 35–40 minutes. Remove from the oven and serve hot.

# Peach and Lemon Verbena Sherbet

10 ripe peaches, peeled, halved, and
    sliced into chunks
1/3 cup chopped fresh lemon
    verbena
1 cup water (or even better, peach
    juice if possible)

1/2 cup sugar
1 tablespoon lemon juice
2 tablespoons peach liqueur
2 cups low-fat buttermilk

6 SERVINGS

1. Place the peaches, lemon verbena, and water (or fruit juice) in a blender or food processor, and blend until evenly pureed. Pour the mixture into a large bowl.

2. Add the remaining ingredients and mix well with a spoon. Pour this mixture into a shallow pan and freeze it for several hours.

3. When ready to serve, cut the sherbet into chunks, and process again until it turns thick and evenly smooth. Remove the sherbet from the blender or food processor, and divide it evenly among six serving dishes. Serve immediately.

# Rustic Omelet with Fruit

(OMELETTE RUSTIQUE AUX FRUITS)

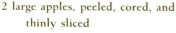
2 large apples, peeled, cored, and thinly sliced
3 pears, peeled, cored, and sliced
7 tablespoons granulated sugar
5 tablespoons Calvados liqueur

6 eggs, separated
A pinch of salt
4 tablespoons (½ stick) sweet butter
Confectioners' sugar, as needed

4 SERVINGS

1. Place the sliced fruit in a deep bowl, add 4 tablespoons of the granulated sugar, and 3 tablespoons of the Calvados liqueur. Toss gently and let it stand for 1 hour.

2. Preheat the oven to 375°.

3. Place the egg yolks in another deep bowl, add the remaining 3 tablespoons granulated sugar and the remaining 2 tablespoons sugar, Calvados. Mix with an electric beater until thick and smooth. In a separate bowl place the egg whites and salt, and beat with the electric beater until they turn stiff and foamy. Gently fold them, in small amounts at a time, into the egg yolk mixture.

4. Just before serving, melt the butter in a large, cast-iron, ovenproof skillet. Pour the egg mixture into it, spread it evenly over the whole skillet, and let it set at the bottom. Smooth the top surface evenly. When the omelet begins to thicken, spread the fruit evenly over the entire top surface. Place the skillet in the oven and bake for about 6–7 minutes, until the top turns golden brown. Dust the top of the omelet with confectioners' sugar, and serve hot. This dessert should always be served hot.

# Raspberry Mousse

1 pint raspberries
1/4 cup granulated sugar
1 1/2 pints heavy cream

1/3 cup confectioners' sugar
4 teaspoons crème de cassis
Small mint leaves, as garnish

4 SERVINGS

1. Wash and trim the raspberries. Place them in a bowl with the 1/4 cup granulated sugar. Toss the ingredients. Let stand for 20 minutes.
2. Place half of the raspberries in a food processor or in a blender. Blend well and place them back in the bowl. With a large sharp knife finely chop the remaining raspberries and add them to the bowl.
3. Whip the cream, confectioners' sugar, and crème de cassis in a previously refrigerated bowl. Whip until the cream turns stiff. Gradually fold the raspberry mixture into the stiff cream. Mix well and refrigerate for at least 3 hours before serving. Garnish the top with small mint leaves.

# Natas (A Portuguese dessert
THAT COMES FROM AN OLD MONASTERY OF NUNS)

1/2 pint heavy cream
2 teaspoons cornstarch
1 cup milk
5 egg yolks

2/3 cup sugar
2 teaspoons orange flavor essence
    (or vanilla extract)
Cinnamon, as garnish

4-6 SERVINGS

1. This dessert should be prepared in a double boiler over low-medium heat.

2. Pour the cream into the top of the double boiler. Dissolve the cornstarch in the milk and add to the cream. In a deep bowl beat the egg yolks and sugar with a mixer and add to the cream. Add the flower essence, or vanilla, or a similar extract.

3. Raise heat to medium and when the water begins to boil, reduce the heat to low-medium. Stir the cream continually until it comes to the boiling point and thickens. Check the seasoning and add more sugar if necessary. When the cream is perfectly smooth and of even consistency, remove it from the heat and pour it into four or six small ramekins. Sprinkle some cinnamon on the top of each ramekin and place them in the refrigerator for several hours before serving.

# Jacob's Pear Flan

1/2 cup all-purpose flour
3/4 cup granulated sugar
One 1/4-ounce package active dry
  yeast
3 eggs, separated
2 cups milk

2 teaspoons vanilla extract
2 ounces (1/2 stick) butter
1/2 pound pears, peeled, cored, and
  thinly sliced
Confectioners' sugar, as garnish

4-6 SERVINGS

1. Preheat the oven to 350°. Place the flour, sugar, and yeast in a deep bowl and mix well. Mix the egg yolks, milk, and vanilla in a separate bowl and add to the flour-sugar mixture. With a mixer blend the ingredients well.

2. Melt the butter in a saucepan and add to the mixture. Again use a mixer to mix the ingredients well.

3. In another bowl, beat the egg whites stiff and gradually fold them into the mixture.

4. Butter thoroughly a long ovenproof dish and gently pour the mixture into it. Distribute the sliced pears over the entire top surface. Place the dish in the oven and bake for about 35–40 minutes. Just before serving, sprinkle some confectioners' sugar on the top as garnish. Serve the flan warm or at room temperature.

# St. Scholastica Peach Tarte

*Pastry Shell (Pâte Brisée)*

1 egg
1 cup flour (half white and half
    whole wheat)
4 ounces (1 stick) butter, cut into
    small pieces

5 tablespoons ice water
A pinch of salt
2 teaspoons sugar

*Filling*

6 peaches, peeled and sliced
2 tablespoons lemon juice

⅓ cup sugar

*Custard Mixture*

2 egg yolks
4 tablespoons sugar

½ cup half-and-half
1 tablespoon peach liqueur

*Topping (Glaze)*

4 tablespoons peach jam
2 tablespoons peach liqueur

1 tablespoon water
1 teaspoon sugar

6 SERVINGS

1. Prepare the pastry shell by mixing all the ingredients in a deep bowl. Use a fork and wet hands for working and mixing the ingredients until they form a dough. Do not overwork the dough. Shape the dough into a ball and place it in the refrigerator for at least 1 hour.
2. Preheat the oven to 250°. Sprinkle flour over a flat surface and carefully roll the dough out, extending it in every direction. Sprinkle a

bit of flour on the top as you roll the dough. Butter thoroughly a tart dish and carefully place the rolled dough in it. Trim the edges, forming some sort of decorative design. Cover the pastry shell with aluminum foil and prebake the shell in the oven for about 12 minutes.

3. While the pastry shell is baking, mix the filling ingredients in a bowl and set aside.

4. Prepare the custard mixture by blending all the ingredients in a bowl with an electric mixer or by hand. Pour the mixture into the pastry shell and place it back into the oven (at the same temperature) for another 8–10 minutes until it sets. Then remove it from the oven. Raise the oven temperature to 350°.

5. Place the reserved peach slices over the set custard following the design of a revolving wheel.

6. In a small nonstick saucepan melt the peach jam, add the liqueur, water, sugar. Stir until the ingredients are well blended. Carefully pour the topping over the peach slices and spread evenly with a brush.

7. Bake about 30 minutes. (If the pastry browns too much cover it with aluminum foil.) Allow it to cool before serving.

# Peach Clafoutis

6 peaches (see Note)
1½ cups milk
4 eggs
½ cup granulated sugar

3 tablespoons peach liqueur (or
    vanilla extract)
Confectioners' sugar, as needed

6 SERVINGS

1. Preheat the oven to 350°.

2. Peel and slice the peaches in perfect halves. Discard the seeds. Set the peaches aside.

3. Prepare the batter by placing the milk, eggs, sugar, and peach liqueur in the blender. Whirl thoroughly at high speed for about 2 minutes.

4. Butter thoroughly a baking dish about 2 inches deep. Pour about one quarter of the batter into the baking dish and place the dish in the oven for about 3 minutes, until the batter has set in the bottom of the dish.

5. Remove the dish from the oven (don't turn off the oven) and spread the peach halves evenly over the batter, the sliced parts down touching the batter. Pour the rest of the batter on the top of the peaches and all around them. Put the dish in the oven and bake for about 35–40 minutes. The clafouti is done when the top begins to puff and turns brown, while the rest remains custardlike. Remove the dish from the oven, sprinkle some confectioners' sugar on the top, both for taste and as garnish. Serve the clafouti warm.

NOTE: If you are pressed for time, you may use canned peach halves for the clafouti. If that is the case, be sure to drain them thoroughly of their juice.

# Apricots Flambé

12 apricots
2 cups water
1/2 cup sugar
A bunch of dried lavender seeds

2 tablespoons apricot liqueur (or peach)
1/2 cup strong rum
Optional: 8 ounces heavy cream (or vanilla ice cream)

6 SERVINGS

1. Wash and carefully peel the apricots. Slice them in perfect halves and then remove the seeds. Set them aside.

2. Place the water in a casserole. Add the sugar, lavender seeds, and liqueur, and bring the liquid to a quick boil. Reduce the heat to low and cover the casserole; continue cooking for another 20 minutes until a syrup is formed.

3. Add the apricots to the syrup and continue cooking over low heat for 12–15 minutes, always with the lid covering the casserole. At the end drain the apricots and set them aside for a few minutes to dry properly. Discard cooking liquid.

4. Just before serving, place the apricots in a large nonstick skillet over medium heat, pour the rum evenly over them, and with a match light the rum. When the flame disappears, the flambé process is done. Serve 4 apricot halves per person, and, if desired, add a touch of cream or ice cream on the top.

# Melon with Strawberry and Raspberry

2 small ripe melons, seeded, peeled
1/4 pound fresh strawberries
1/4 pound fresh raspberries

1/2 cup granulated sugar
1/2 cup sweet red vermouth
2 tablespoons lemon juice

*Sauce*

One 12-ounce container low-fat
   plain yogurt

1/2 cup confectioners' sugar, more if
   desired
3 tablespoons crème de cassis

4-6 SERVINGS

1. Slice the melons in even slices lengthwise. Wash and trim the strawberries and the raspberries. Carefully place them in a large elongated dish. Try to distribute the fruits evenly. Sprinkle the sugar over them evenly.

2. In a bowl, mix the vermouth and lemon juice and pour evenly over the fruit. Place the dish in the refrigerator for at least 2 hours until ready to be served.

3. Place the yogurt in a deep bowl. Add the confectioners' sugar and crème de cassis. Blend well with an electric mixer and refrigerate until ready to serve.

4. Divide the melon slices among 4–6 serving dishes. Form a six-pointed star with them, leaving space in between the slices. Place some strawberries and raspberries in the spaces. Place a big scoop of the yogurt sauce at the center and serve.

# Index